THIRSTING HEARTS

by
Carolyn Solomon

ISBN: 0-75962-353-8

This book is printed on acid free paper.

1stBooks – rev. 05/08/01

CHAPTER 1
(1886)

"What god gave men all the power?" Imogene Washington demanded to know from her seat inside the box buggy pulling before the abode on Canfield Street, an affluent Negro section of town.

Laughter echoed into evening's quiet.

"Nobody gave them any such thing. Men have always taken what they want... . They are the stronger sex," she added derisively, still stewing from a recent disagreement with a pompous male.

Laughter rang out again as Imogene and her companion jumped from the buggy onto frozen ground.

"Careful, Maude!" Imogene cried. Her naked hand upon the buggy saved her companion from falling.

"Take your own advice, Immie dear," Maude replied.

Hand in hand, Imogene and her friend, Maude Graves, mounted stairs and skidded toward the entrance. They giggled. One would have thought children played upon the porch instead of two adults.

"Hurry!" Maude shouted, holding doors open.

Sliding cape from her shoulders, Imogene placed the outer garment upon a coat hook. Rubbing her frosty hands together, she followed Maude into a familiar room. Golden warmth from the fireplace elevated her mood. A favorite seat beckoned. She melded into pink-flowered cushions. "Perfect fit," she sighed.

Maude, her ally of twenty years, called out something, incoherent. Unconcerned with her friend's muffled chatter, she luxuriated in comfort and warmth. Her still chilled hands rested in her woolen skirts. I'll have to mend this tear, she reminded herself. Fingers smoothed a small hole in her brown dress while she awaited Maude's return.

Flames drew her attention and conjured memories of when Mother lived, and Father's concerns cemented the Washington family. Fifteen years ago her life had resembled Maude's when the seamstress had outfitted them with current attire. Footwear, underthings and such were replaced, at least, annually. When odors of honey and tea invaded those reveries, she reached for a silver tray in Maude's slender hands. Gold-edged china, silverware and a clear jar of honey, glistening like liquid gold, distracted and nearly caused her to upset the tray.

"Just take your cup, Immie!"

At Maude's autocratic tones, she only smiled. She'd grown used to her companion acting like an elder sister. "You're truly a dear friend, Maude," she purred.

"Don't get sentimental on me, Immie. You make me feel ancient." Maude's long fingers patted her thick black mane, and her lips spread in a self-conscious smile. "I don't need reminders of my thirty-seven years to your twenty-five."

"With age comes success and wisdom." Imogene was truly grateful for her ally and meant no harm.

"Not always." Maude seemed to regain some composure as one hand lowered. It laid perfectly poised and dark against her lace covered bosom. "Speaking of success, I'm more than happy with yours. Soon, Immie dear, you'll champion our rights. Like Susan B Anthony, you'll travel, spread 'the word', raise much needed funds and achieve as much as she. Astounding is the only word I can give to your progress and performance."

She could only beam with pride from Maude's words. Tingling china; scents of honey flavored tea; and general feelings of comfort coaxed additional contentment. She was blessed in having Maude Graves, a renowned Negro suffragette, as her instructor and colleague.

"I fear, we, as Negro women, will need more cohorts. Many white females embrace this cause that's so pertinent to us all. But I fear that may eventually change. If there's ever question about racial differences, you and I know what road our white sisters will take. We must be prepared." Maude's alto trailed off.

"You're correct. We must be ready; stalwart as solders," Imogene affirmed. She watched her ally walk towards flowing curtains. Lace panels fluttered from a partially opened window and resembled white winged apparitions caught in the breeze.

"It's late, Immie. You're welcome to spend the night."

"I would love to stay, but I can't." She stood, accepting help with her outerwear. Pulling its gray hood securely over her locks, she silently cursed shoulder-length hair that, resembled Father's sandy-colored unruly mane. Because Maude insisted Imogene's ungovernable locks denoted individuality and distinguished her from other women orators, Imogene never considered altering her hair.

"Take care, Immie," Maude admonished, leading her outside.

"I will," she replied, moving from her friend's supporting grip and easing toward her buggy.

Gas lamps lit tree-lined streets and palatial-looking homes in that section of Detroit. Those who lived here were from families of established backgrounds with "old" money. Her family would have been, if not for Father's frivolities, so favored. Pushing such thoughts aside, her taller than average frame leaned, and she hastened the horse forward. Hague Street appeared. Thoughts turned to Mother and the supporting comfort she had given ... but that was gone. Those memories were pushed aside; others, more current and urgent, surfaced.

After harboring horse and buggy, she mounted snow-covered steps and rushed inside the house. If he were home, they could share a cozy dinner.

"Father?" she called.

He did not answer, and she feared current rumors might be true. Was he gambling again? How? They barely had money from his menial jobs for food. And her small savings accumulated from doing odd sewing was not at his disposal—they were with Maude. Placing cape upon the empty coat rack, she sailed into the kitchen. He might arrive in time and join her for supper.

Embers smoldered in the stove's belly, and foods, cooked earlier, remained as she'd left them. Corn bread, string beans and fried chicken still looked appetizing, but they held no appeal for her. Concern if Father had resumed gambling, and what collateral he used, were more paramount. She sighed; left the kitchen's warmth and trudged upstairs to an unheated room.

She undressed in the chill; washed with ice-encrusted water from the chipped porcelain bowl and donned her worn sleep wear. Burrowing in once colorful quilts—they still gave comfort and warmth, reminding her of Mother—Imogene prepared for sleep. Her beloved matriarch had spent final sickness between the quilt's threadbare folds. Like a babe wrapped in her mother's essence, Imogene slumbered.

***

Seth Thomas stood near a window of the home located on Second Avenue. He, owner of the three-story building, focused from drifting snow outside to observe two men inside, sitting at the gaming table. He approached an elder man who persisted in ignoring him.

"Bill!" he shouted, placing a hand upon the old-timer's chair, hoping to draw the man's heed. His fingers slid from the velvet upholstery and rested upon the oldster's worn shirt.

The man raised his white head, an obsessed expression, wild like his shoulder-length mane, in his hazel eyes.

"Come, Mr. Washington, you must leave." Caressing the chair's smoothness, somehow, aided his composure as he spoke softly and gave Bill a wrinkled tail coat. But the elder knocked the garment from his hand. It lay upon the new carpet like a dirt spot.

"Deal the cards, Frank!" the geezer shouted.

"Well, Seth?" Frank Kossel, held cards between claw-like fingers and sought permission from his boss and friend.

"Take your winnings—" Seth said to Bill, not responding to his partner. "Go home!" His voice reverberated more than usual and not because of its natural deep tones. Determination to be rid of such a mule-headed man prompted his voice's pitch.

4

"No! I came here with much more. I'll not leave with anything less." Bill shook his untamed mane and stared at the playing cards in Frank's hands.

Viewing Bill Washington with as much disgust as pity, Seth nodded to his ally. Having no desire to witness the man's inevitable downfall, he walked away before the hands were dealt.

Strolling from confrontation; down the long corridor, he lavished in relative quiet. But absence only made him dwell more on Bill Washington. He vowed the crazed man would never grace his establishment again. Why didn't the demented fool just count losses and leave?

An exclusive men's club must remain just that, preferential and unsullied. Only influential gents had frequented his place. For substantial fees members had a safe, discreet place for diversion and recreation. The club offered male camaraderie, billiards and cards in an atmosphere of smoking and moderate drinking. Seth tolerated, he did not encourage, the few members who always brought female companions.

"Seth!" Repetitive thumps echoed down the hall. "I need you!"

He turned. Urgency on Frank's lean face—paler than usual—dissolved his reveries.

"Bill's offering his house." Frank acted as if he'd struck gold.

"No!" Seth said unequivocally. Some things were best avoided like property, heirlooms and disagreeable women. They could wreck havoc with everyone involved.

"Why not?" Frank pleaded. "If he's fool enough—"

"No! You know that's not my policy." His stance widened.

"We can exchange it for cash; let it draw interest."

"Never, Frank. Mr. Washington must leave now." He advanced towards the gaming room. A gun's barrel met him as he entered the space. Instinctively he froze and raised his hands.

"Heard you, Mr. Thomas," Bill spewed. "I only want a chance at winning back what I lost." Still holding the gun, he thrust a folded document into Seth's face. "I lose, it's yours."

5

"If you listened, then you know my answer's no." He lowered his hand, slipping them into his knicker pockets. He gave silent thanks that his opponent had not noticed. His gaze alternated from the gun in his face to Bill's eyes, brimming, it seemed, with desperation.

"You either give me the chance to win back all my money or else." Bill flung the document near coins and bills stacked upon the table. Hell-bent, the man stepped back.

A shot rung out. Frank fell back into the oak-paneled wall.

"Don't move, Mr. Thomas. He ain't hurt."

Frank maintained his fallen position and the stunned look upon his lean face.

"Next time I'll aim for his heart, not his Stetson." Bill's grin disappeared into his overgrown whiskers.

"Deal the cards, Frank," Seth instructed. He would accept defeat ... for now.

His partner rose, inspecting damage done to his white hat. Frank's baby finger protruded through a singed hole in the hat. Once he'd settled in a chair, with the headgear covering his greased black hair, he shuffled the playing cards.

Seth slid into a seat indicated by Bill's waving firearm. He eased a hand into his pocket, but gut feelings kept him from withdrawing the Derringer there. He'd have to kill or seriously wound Bill. What other way was there to stop such craziness? He had friends in high places; so did Bill. His family could ill-afford adverse attention. Placing both hands upon the table, he decided to let this play out.

The game progressed with Frank dealing and playing his own hand. Seth took instructions from Bill regarding the other hand while the old man gripped his weapon.

Deal after deal, hour followed hour, the men played cards doled out. Bill's document and the few coins he still had were wagered against the house's reserves. The senior had early wins. Fate was tempted long enough; tables turned. In a matter of minutes Bill lost all profits; they accumulated upon stacked currency near Frank's elbow. The senior, without hesitation, threw in his deeds.

Only an insane man would do that, Seth thought.

Frank exposed a joker, four aces and a triumphant grin.

"It's over." Seth threw in the hand played at Bill's directive. He stood. A sigh seeped from between his clenched teeth as he hoped his tormentor would finally leave.

The elder appeared frantic. His hands tensed, making already prominent veins even more pronounced. His finger twitched around the trigger.

Seth slid a hand in his pocket for the Derringer.

But the vanquishing elder's furrowed features twisted and froze. His thin bulk convulsed once, twice, three times. Cards, coins paperbacks spewed about the table and spilled into carpet fibers. Bill's arms dangled over the stockpile he'd strove to win. Ultimately, it had destroyed him. As if in announcement, the deeds sailed off the table. Momentarily, it hovered above scattered currency and drifted to the floor.

"I don't need trouble. Get the authorities, Frank." Seth said uneasily.

Lost in thought, it seemed Frank had gone and returned in a heartbeat. Customary greetings were given the coroner, physician and undertaker as they began their various tasks.

"We must stake our claim," Frank indicated, interrupting Seth's observations.

"Has Bill family?" Frowning from his partner's concern over "material things", Seth ignored the man's statement and had questioned the undertaker, Mr. Johnson.

"Yes," the man responded.

"We must talk." Seth pulled Frank into an adjoining room. "Close the door," he called over his shoulder.

"What's there to talk about?" Frank remained near the exit.

"There's more at stake here than monetary gain." Seth had perched upon the spacious desk. He silenced his cohort by shaking his head. "My family's name; our honor are in jeopardy."

"You can't cancel the man's debt!" Frank moved from the door and stood eye level with Seth's seated figure.

"Of course I can. Only you and I know. Bill's dead. We'll inadvertently return the deed to this relation of his. No one need know."

"I told them." Frank pointed toward the gaming room where the three men worked.

Seth frowned in disapproval.

"Had to give reasons," Frank gushed.

"Still doesn't matter, Seth responded after some thought.

"But ..."

"I can't evict anyone's family. We'll work out something."

"Why?"

"Forget it, Frank. I've decided," he said, standing. "Since the word's out, we'll have to get to Bill's family and state our position. Let's go and get it over with."

Well-protected from the elements, in bowler, muffler and cape overcoat, Seth mounted his stallion. Side by side, he and his ally rode. Into the night and through deserted streets, they ventured. They came upon the house number given them by Mr. Johnson mid-way Hague Street. The ill-kept two-story home broadcasted either its inhabitant's laziness or lack of finance, and those realizations only made him more determined to not enforce the eviction.

No response came from his gloved hand knocking upon the door.

"No one's home." Frank stood behind him.

He pounded harder upon the entrance.

Inside remained unlit and quiet.

"Where could they be at this unholy hour?" he bellowed, pounding repeatedly.

"I'm coming," sounded from inside the enclosure. Light floated pass one thinly draped window. The portal creaked open.

"Holy Mother!" Seth exclaimed. He beheld a thinly-clad creature. His eyes traveled over the person's naked feet to rest upon hazel orbs and shoulder-length mane which reminded him of that crazed-eye, wild-haired man; the cause of his distress. He uttered, "Bill Washington ..."

"In a gentler, kinder, less destructive version," he heard Frank say, snickering, just as the female shrieked and commenced slamming the door in their faces.

CHAPTER 2

At such a late hour, only Father could have been at the door. He often returned at this time. Sleepily, she turned the key in the lock, but before fully opening the entrance, she'd noticed a strange man standing there. Quick wit had prompted her to slam the door shut, but a black gloved hand had thrust the access wide. If she'd not jumped back, surely, she would have suffered great bodily harm.

A towering figure entered, maintaining a position that blocked any means of escape outside to summon the neighbors. The unexpected visitor and cold caused Imogene to draw the red flowered shawl, hastily thrown across her shoulders, shut. She feared the flimsy material might emphasize more than hide her womanliness. When the dark intruder pushed his bowler back, she believed for a better view, her hand tightened, and naturally pulled the covering closer to her form.

"Sorry for this unannounced visit," he said in deep tones that denoted command. "Bill Washington is your relation?"

As the shadowy figure moved near, she found disfavor with him even before he'd indicated the purpose for his intrusion. He loomed over her—many men she stood eye level with or not far below. His outerwear accented already broad shoulders. That offensive gloved hand pushed the hat farther off his dark features and loosened a red muffler from his broad neck.

Black eyes studied her just as intently as she examined him. His face, the deepest brown, displayed well-chiseled and strong traits. He was Negro, but one distinct aspect, Asian eyes, caused her doubt. Deep indentations at the corners of his upper lips weren't evidence of a smile. A wide hawkish nose and small gold earring conjured memories of pirates, plundering and capturing anything: riches ... women ... her ...

Something, someone, behind the unwelcomed caller moved. Did he have an accomplice?

She screamed and jumped back.

A slightly shorter man brushed past and approached the fireless hearth. Warmth was not what he sought. He poked at and fingered her most treasured objects: figurines and family portraits. By today's standards, these things were of dubious monetary value.

"What is he doing?" she uttered, speaking to herself.

"I haven't introduced myself, Miss ..."

She swung around, facing the taller of the two men.

"I'm Seth Thomas and this is my partner, Frank Kossel." His ebony eyes remained on the Stetson-hatted man.

She watched Kossel abandon his inspection and come closer. A crooked smiled accompanied his nod of acknowledgment. She gave no response other than eyeing Thomas. Wasn't he the dominant one in this affair? She studied his sloe eyes and silently questioned the unease dwelling there.

"Bill's had an accident," his partner said.

"My father?" she gyrated between the two men.

The lighter-complexioned man opened his mouth to speak while retrieving something from his pocket. Large knuckled fingers began unfolding a brownish paper.

"No, Frank! That can wait," Thomas directed.

But Imogene captured the parchment before Kossel could return it to his pocket. A quick glance indicated the document as hers. Thomas took the certificate from her unsuspecting grip.

"Miss, we'll work out some agreement regarding this." He held the contract in a gloved hand. "Perhaps you should sit."

Tired of all the mystery, she released her shawl. It fell, lying like discarded red flowers at her tormentor's feet as she stood toe to toe with him.

"What have you done to my father?" she demanded.

The stranger who loomed over her could have, with one stroke, pushed her aside. But that neither frightened nor altered confrontation with this dark man. Unblinking, she held his black eyes and her stance.

"He's dead," her enemy's crony interjected.

The import of Kossel's too blunt statement coupled with his highly impersonal tone made her lose ground. She swayed, fell back; hands upon her forearms guided her to the horsehair sofa. An object sailed to the floor as she sunk into the lumpy cushions. Her brain felt near exploding as her head plummeted to her quivering palms. She fought and nearly lost the battle to suppress resulting sobs and convulsions. When her throbbing head finally lifted, she noticed Seth Thomas crouched at face level.

This bearer of bad news, rested a gloved hand upon hers. How dare he! She pushed his hand—the offending extremity—away.

His agile form rose and loomed over her.

No coward, Imogene sprung up. Her bare feet postured before Seth's laced shoes. "You evil man. What—what nefarious deed have you done to my father?"

His silence, she saw as arrogance and male superiority. It was too easy to vent anger and frustration on him and his attitude. He embodied, so well, the all-powerful selfish male. From what had occurred, no one could tell her Seth Thomas was not the controlling force in this situation, and his partner only followed instructions.

Slight attention reflected upon Frank retrieving an item from the floor near her naked feet. Only when he handed the paper to Thomas did she recognize her deed. The swiftness of that gloved hand aborted any attempt at capturing the prize.

"You—you pompous, officious ass," she cried out in frustration.

From behind, Frank snickered.

But her attention stayed on Seth Thomas, the person she saw as her opponent. His composure appeared unchanged. But she heard and felt the bite in his voice.

"You do not know me, Miss. So on what do you base that assumption?"

She flushed.

He stood, waiting patiently, for her to explain what she found so obvious.

"Why I—I ..." Imogene stammered. She had always found the right words to say. And why should she clarify her outbursts of truth? "The deed is mine!"

That bad news messenger's deep voice softened, but remained certain. "We must come to some agreement—in writing—before I can return this to you."

He represented, too well the self-possessed physically stronger sex and made her only too aware of her own limitations and the sudden lost of her father, the remaining link with her ancestry. Overwhelming aloneness surrounded her.

"Can we—I get a neighbor or friend to come over?"

She did not respond and blocked out anything else her foe might have said.

Only when the dark intruder and his ally left, only then, did she release pent-up emotions. No solace came. Even warmth from her own arms about her trembling body helped little.

She bemoaned the fact that Father would never return. His faults—so insignificant at this moment—she did not lament over, but his presence, important now and forever, she felt. Moans echoed through the house as her heart seemed near bursting and her head pounded. Hammering sounded as if coming from the door too. Listening carefully, she approached the noise.

Had he returned? How dare he interrupt her anguish! With renewed valor she snatched the portal open, ready for battle. Hadn't he caused enough grief and mischief?

"Immie! I came as soon as I heard."

"Maude!" she fell into her friend's outstretched arms, relieved and thankful.

"Mr. Thomas said you needed someone."

She lifted her head from Maude's shoulder and glimpsed a shadow through dawn's haze. The silhouette seemed a man—her enemy? He turned away and rode off, fading into distance.

***

13

After having spent time with Maude and her parents, boosted by their comfort and offer of help, Imogene had attempted sleep. But she soon rose from the warmth of covers. Present conditions allowed neither rest nor leisure. Much needed her attention.

Father required burying—an expense she could ill afford. Employment and cheap housing were equally important. She had declined the Graves' offer of residence, because they would never accept compensation, and she could not keep intruding upon their friendship.

After dressing and cleaning the guest room she'd occupied, Imogene gave farewells and departed. Assaulting winds made her pull woolen cloak closer about her body and head while she boarded the vehicle. One matter demanded attention now. At its completion, she could proceed with Father's burial, seeking gainful employment and renting suitable residence.

Fortified and determined she rode through the semi-quiet streets of Detroit. A white brick, three-story building towered in the distance. Green scrolled pillars loomed upwards and met, it seemed, gray skies. Often she'd passed this place labeled the Thomas Mansion. It felt strange visiting the place or associating with the home's occupants. Their great wealth had not been the reason for her feelings, but illegal activity held there had prompted that impression.

After several taps with the boar's head knocker and much prancing around for warmth, to Imogene's relief, double doors opened. But her joy at some ease from the cold proved fleeting.

A white-aproned figure, unsmiling, blocked the entrance and offered no admittance or words of welcome.

"Mr. Thomas, please," Imogene said, ignoring the older woman's rudeness.

"Which one?"

Before she responded, a slightly familiar voice asked, "Who is it, Ola?"

Seth Thomas's assistant appeared. The man reached over the servant's squat form and directed Imogene into a big foyer.

"I'm here regarding my house," she declared.

He cocked one eyebrow, staring at her in unresponsiveness, while he fumbled with something in his trouser pocket.

"I must see Mr. Thomas," she affirmed, growing agitated with the indifference she'd received from him and his servant.

"He's indisposed now."

She took the man's continued smugness as implied dismissal. He would not dissuade her! And she had no intention of returning at Seth Thomas's convenience.

"Sir," she said, having forgotten his name.

"Frank Kossel," he replied mocking, not making any effort at getting his boss.

"I'm not leaving." She could be just as stubborn. "Whatever Mr. Thomas is doing can't be more important than this issue of my home," again, she affirmed.

"The house is legally ours," he insisted. "No one coerced Bill into betting the property. In fact, we tried to dissuade the fool"

"You need me, Frank?" A remembered voice sounded, staying angry words she would have said at reference to her father.

Facing that commanding voice, she recognized Thomas as he approached, moving like some dark creature. A long silk robe outlined his well-built body; his black hair shown trimmed and wet. Savory essence remained after he had strolled past.

"In here, Miss Washington." He stepped back from the portal and permitted Imogene to enter.

Once in the sitting room, she stood and observed her surroundings. Blends of greens and yellows welcomed, making her feel refreshed. Never had she encountered such opulence in furnishings, carpets or art objects. It felt as if cooling waters had swept over her, washing all disturbances away. But she came here for a fight, if necessary, with the dark male who had affected her life so adversely.

Seth stood facing away from her. He had opened mint-green drapes and seemed engrossed upon something or someone outside.

Her eyes were glued upon his towering presence. She could not help but notice how the robe's smoothness clothed his broad shoulders, taunt middle and narrow hips.

"Might I have your cape?" Frank interrupted.

Imogene shut gapping lips and started rubbing still chilled hands. Sweeping aside embarrassment and the man's mocking smile, she thanked him and took a seat.

Before she fully recovered composure or really settled into the flowered chair's comfort, Ola, the sour-faced servant, appeared. Fresh coffee wafted through the room and teased her senses. Once Ola deposited the silver tray of brew, sugar and creme with china and utensils upon a side table, the rotund servant left without a word or offer of assistance. Imogene frowned in displeasure.

"You may help yourself, Miss Washington," Seth Thomas said as he settled in an adjoining chair.

Her foe's dark eyes watched too intently. Seeking diversion, she reached for the coffee container. It weighed like steel. Praying he had not noticed her trembling hands, she poured the steaming brew. When directed to her lips, the hot drink slopped at the cup's rim. Sheer willpower steadied her hand. Weakness, in any form, could only defeat. But holding his stare and focusing upon the drink, proved difficult. The swallow she took burnt both tongue and throat. Why had she not added cream and sugar? She always had before.

"You all right?" he asked, His lips, well-formed, quivered, threatening, she was certain, a smile.

Looking from his face should have ended discomfort. It had not. Her eyes kept straying to his state of dress, or, more accurately, the man's state of undress. What had she expected? His assistant had said he was unavailable. Not wanting to, she admitted having done a foolish thing. Well, it didn't matter now. She would assert her position and be done with it. But instead of indicating the purpose for this visit, her thoughts and gaze kept drifting back to Thomas. Was he naked under the robe's silken folds? Answer came when one muscular leg uncovered from mid-thigh to bare foot. He had moved forward in his chair.

"Sweet treat, Miss Washington?"

Her eyes adverted and opened lips shut. A plate of sugary confections were offered. After selecting an iced bun; keeping it between two fingers, she inspected the presenter and smiled appreciation. Because her tormentor's silent stare and garb still spawned disquiet, she felt some security with another there, even if her enemy's colleague.

"Mr. Thomas, I'm here about my property," she asserted, still holding the bun between two fingers.

"I know," he said, making no attempt to cover his exposed limb.

Either the expression on Seth's handsome face or his voice, both cocksure, conjured visions of the "mighty" male, making her recall other domineering man she'd had conflicts with.

"Are you certain of my position about the house and deed?"

"Your partner told me," she said, wondering why Seth shot his ally hostile looks. Or had the action been meant for her?

"I've not discussed the matter fully with him yet. You should know that I'm willing to let you remain in the—your home—after we come to a written agreement."

She did not answer right away because attention dwelled upon his white, manicured nails and how they complimented the sable hue of his bare knee. But once realizing what an agreement might entail with a man, very possibly, involved with Father's death, she declared, "Contract? Written? And for what? You have my deed and your accomplice's verification. Which amounts, in any fool's opinion, as nothing!"

For several minutes, Seth's long fingers toyed with his uncovered knee as he looked from her to Frank. "If not for an indiscretion, there would have been no need for any interchange between me and you."

She listened closely and wondered why this affluent man had permitted her father, without benefit of membership, entry into his exclusive club?

As if he had heard her silent query, Seth said, "The only reason I allowed Bill Washington here was because of his friend, John Graves. He's an established respected member. Bill, your father, often came with him."

"Mr. Graves witnessed the whole incident?" If such proved true, she felt that gave more credence to Seth Thomas's claim of ownership. Disappointment fell over her features.

"No, John always leaves near ten."

She smiled in triumph.

"The whole affair's on record with authorities."

"Of course, you would protect your interests." She frowned, disheartened.

"That doesn't have to be a problem, Miss Washington. We can make an agreement for your protection and concern."

"Your concern, you mean!" Did he think her a fool?

He didn't respond, in fact, he appeared frustrated. His black eyes searched her face. Finally, he continued, "It'll benefit us both. But, then, would you or I suffer greater harm from lost of your home?"

"He could have stated it no better. She did have the most to lose. But that neither lessened her anger nor stopped her from viewing Seth's assertion as a cocky display of male superiority that dripped with ulterior motives.

"Let's make this official." A typed parchment laid in his hands. "You sign ..."

"I have no intention ..."

"Miss Washington, hear me out, please."

She listened, but not with an opened mind.

"Eviction isn't my aim. You may stay in your home."

"Under what conditions?" she said, discounting explanation; believing his motives ulterior. "Nothing's free. I'm no child!"

His gaze swept over her form. "And I'm not blind. I see you're a woman ... full grown."

Had he given insult or compliment? Imogene shifted, uneasy, in her chair. The uneaten sugar bun slipped from her fingers into the almost empty coffee cup. She prayed her adversary had not noticed her muffled cry of surprise or the mishap.

"If you read—" His face revealed only earnestness shaded with impatience. "You'll find the terms favorable."

"For you!" She stood, more for impact than anything else.

"You're mistaken." His deep voice sounded more insistent.

"I will neither read nor accept your proposal!"

"Adjustments can be made. Look the form over." He thrust the writ at her. The man's curt actions belied his soft timbre.

"I will not!" She saw anger mounting in his eyes, but would not quiet her biting tongue. "You have covered your tracks well, sir. And I'm at a disadvantage ... for now."

The sight of her worn cape draped across Frank's extended arm interrupted. Its gently swaying bottom signaled departure time. She hadn't called for the wrap. Why had he brought it?

Seth rose. His long robe concealed the previously exposed leg. "You misunderstand, Miss Washington."

"I haven't time for argument. Other matters call." Father's funeral came to mind.

"Mr. Johnson has Bill's body," Seth commented.

Her mouth opened in awe. How could he have known what she thought? Eerie sensations beset, and she felt need for flight.

"I must leave." She accepted the outerwear held open by his assistant. Without further words, she rushed outdoors and boarded the buggy. Safe from the dark male who invoked images of earringed sea robbers, Imogene prided herself upon evading his obvious offer of an evil arrangement. Powerful men were known to presume unfortunates, especially women, ripe and easy victims for their wickedness. Yes, she had bested him!

***

"Now we know she's neither a gentler nor kinder version of Bill," Frank said as he examined the confection in his hand.

For over fifteen years he and Frank had coexisted, and their combined efforts had contributed to success. Disagreements had come, as in any partnership, but they had remained loyal, never letting anything keep them divided.

"Why didn't she have a man or lawyer tend this matter?" Seth asked, frustrated.

"She probably feels able as any man." Frank wrapped wide lips around the sweet bun. "Women like her pride themselves upon independence from men."

"I'm not asking for her bondage," Seth spewed, feeling he should let the woman boil in her own stubbornness and suspend further offers of help. All his concern she'd rejected. And, like her father, Bill, she'd not listened, but had remained hell-bent upon some other agenda.

"You were too accommodating. Why? She's not frail-looking like your intended, Johnetta. She's almost my six feet height."

Seth more than agreed. But concern for and uneasiness with the woman's present circumstances still troubled him.

"Miss Washington's a woman alone now. And the property's lost or gain, won't really alter our wealth," he said.

"Did we ask for the house?" Frank licked icing from his skinny fingers. "She, like any woman, can get money or shelter for sexual favors."

"True, but that doesn't make me proud causing her to resort to such measures. What if she hasn't any appreciation for men?"

"Doubt that," Frank snickered. "I saw how she watched you."

He hadn't noticed. But Seth knew his body's appeal—too many women had praised his physical attributes. Still he felt Miss Washington despised him fully. Weren't her words and actions proof enough?

"Her eyes were glued to your backside, and her lips hung open." Frank laughed indecently. "My, my. You must have looked like rare steak to her."

"Wake me at four, Frank." Usually his friend's familiar chuckle lightened Seth's mood, but not this time. Barefoot, he strolled down the hall. The dressing coat's smoothness gliding over his nakedness invoked memories of Miss Washington. He'd been long without a woman. Is that why her light hazel eyes—haughty and matching Bill's burning looks—still appealed?

Unease continued as he entered his darkened rooms. Quiet warmth enveloped as he laid naked beneath soft covers. But sleep and comfort eluded. Troubling feelings taunted. He tossed, suspended between awareness and unconsciousness. Visions floated in his head.

A tall, determined woman pervaded his thoughts. Moderately broad nose, freckled skin and fleshly lips enhanced the allure. Thick sandy hair—so unlike the females he knew who wore theirs in shinny ringlets or waves—was shoulder length like Bill's unruly mass, even if she had pulled it into one thick braid behind her unadorned ears.

"Seth!"

His eyes unsealed. Brightness flooded darkness. Frank stood near drawn drapes.

Had he slept? Where had time gone? He must prepare for evening's activities. Chills came when he slipped from bed's warmth and left as he secured the robe over his nakedness. Thoughts cleared; he knew now why he had tolerated the woman's stubborn indifference to his more than generous offer.

"Somehow, I feel ..."

"What?" Frank asked before exiting.

"Miss Washington, I feel responsible for the woman."

"Humph," Frank rasped, his usual accompanying titter absent, before he left, slamming the door.

CHAPTER 3

Imogene experienced deep melancholy and crying bouts before accepting her father's death. Once she reconciled his permanent absence, there remained problems of getting gainful employment and safe residence for herself, a lone female. It mattered not that Seth Thomas had offered unlimited occupancy. The home, she now admitted, was lawfully his, and she hated owing her sworn enemy anything.

Many affluent Negroes lived and operated businesses in a section of Detroit. She knew most of those merchants and felt her chances for work good. This morning she would seek a job. So attired in Sunday's best—black bustled dress adorned with white cuffs and collar; spit-polished "Barrette" boots—she studied her image in the hall mirror a third time. Passing inspection, she donned gray cape, exited and boarded her buggy.

Pulling before Mr. Pott's general store, she secured her buggy and stepped assuredly into the small establishment. Bells tingled above the door, announcing entry. Wood, coal and sawdust teased her nostrils. Stifling an urge to sneeze, she searched the place. Bolts of colorful, stacked material caught her eye. Sacked foods, barrels and cooking utensils drew little notice. With chilled hands she removed hood, brushing stray hairs from eyes and face.

"Miss Imogene, how you doin'?" A bald head popped up, like jack in the box, from behind a mountain of yellow fabric. Mr. Pott's greeting spilled from his grinning, toothless mouth.

Remaining near the red-bellied stove and rubbing hands for warmth, Imogene fought surfacing displeasure and remembered unpleasantness. Why had she sought this man for help? And he the very person brought home by Father for a prospective suitor. Hadn't she openly and continually rejected the elder? Would he now return her disfavor?

"Sorry 'bout Bill?"

"Thank you, Mr. Potts." His sincere voice dispelled any nasty memories of their former encounters. She smiled back.

"Can I be of service to you, Miss Imogene?"

At closer inspection, the owner's leering gaze and grin caused uneasiness, making her seriously think of forsaking this needed task. But work as suffragist had prepared her for adversity. Surely, the friendship Mr. potts had shared with her father counted and would buy gainful employment.

"Yes," the oldster said, simpering.

"I need work," she forced out.

"Need a cook," he replied, eyeing her like some special delight. "Would be nice—" Wrinkles around his hairy lips deepened, making him look clownish. "You to clean my house and warm my bed ..."

"Oh no! I need honest duties." She stressed the word honest, distancing from his approach.

"What's more legal than being my wife?" He kept advancing.

"Wife?" She froze.

"Yes, Mrs. Imogene Potts." The old man beamed, making his lined features appear even more clownish.

"You misunderstand, Mr. Potts. I'm still not interested in being your dutiful, insignificant spouse. Fair work for good pay is what I want."

"That's well and fine." He continued approaching.

She smiled, pleased and relieved he finally understood.

"My dear, you can cook, clean and share my bed without benefit of marriage." He patted her shoulder. "I'll pay well."

Before her outrage exploded, bells jingled, announcing an entry. She marveled at the dramatic change in the owner. The stupid grin faded from his lips and lust fell from his eyes, changing into utmost respect.

"Mr. Johnson, good day. At your service, sir."

Recognizing the caretaker's stern face—the tall man always dressed in black—Imogene remembered not paying Father's funeral expenses. Even though she'd not received an invoice, in all fairness, it required payment. Perhaps Mr. Johnson had overlooked the debt and its mailing. Once he concluded his business, she planned on giving reason for not settling the debt sooner.

Mr. Johnson's errand involved purchasing an anniversary gift—no matter the cost—for his wife, Alma.

Imogene watched the proprietor's elderly body acquire unexpected agility. He brought forth two gold encrusted bottles from a locked compartment. Both opened containers he held under Mr. Johnson's beak nose. After sniffing each fragrance, the customer stepped back. He appeared puzzled and unable to decide between either scent. Mr. Potts stood, offering no suggestions.

A perfect opportunity! Imogene recognized both phials by sight, and she knew which one the most affluent would buy.

Long ago, during happier days, Lilly, her mother, had worn JASMINE, the most favored perfume. Before Father gambled their riches, he always purchased no other costly bouquet for Mother.

"Might I assist you, Mr. Johnson?" Smiling, Imogene approached the men. Realizing she could prove her worth as an employee, she added, "This fragrance every woman craves. Few can afford it." Her fingers caressed the crystal bottle in the tall man's slender hands. "Any woman would deem this French bouquet apt expression of love. Mr. Petway's wife wears no other fragrance. Having done personal sewing for her, I do know."

When the caretaker reached under his clothing, produced and counted necessary moneys, Imogene smiled—mentioning Mr. Petway, Mr. Johnson's white competitor, she knew would cinch the deal.

"Mr. Potts, you have an asset in this young woman." He'd mistaken her for an employee. Usual austerity left his lean face. He presented the most solicitous look that transformed his features handsome. "You're Bill's daughter?" The slim man appeared concerned. "So sorry about your father."

After thanking the undertaker for his regard and certain he would question her delay at paying burial costs, she offered, "I will settle Father's funeral expenses when ..."

"Accept my apology for sending the invoice," he expressed puzzlement.

"I never received one, but ..."

"Good." Mr. Johnson secured the wrapped package and rushed towards the exit.

"I'll pay ..." She ran after his disappearing figure. Her voice mingled with tingling bells above the shop's exit.

"The bill's been paid." He had turned. His angular features hung between concern and impatience. As if she were a child with an unimportant problem, he walked away.

"Who?" she called. That generous person must be repaid.

Not stopping, he said, "Young lady, don't worry about it."

His authoritarian look and voice silenced her, and she gave little heed to another's question.

"Miss Imogene, what's your price?"

Remembering her earlier mission, she gave Mr. Potts a dismissive look—she'd no time for indecent proposals. Turning upon her heels, Imogene did not respond and melded with outdoor traffic. Her boots beat across the road where mounds of manure assailed the senses.

"Miss Imogene, didn't you hear me?" shouted from behind.

"Mr. Potts." She rotated in anger. "I had believed you, an old family friend, would give me honest employment." Dismissing the elder's attempted interruption, she continued with, "But you proved me wrong." Sudden rush and sting of cold winds stopped further words and hasten her departure.

"Wait, dea—Miss Imogene. The job's yours."

She had heard the merchant's offer, but ignored it. Why subject herself to this man's added abuse? His degrading offer would never cease. Other employment could be found in town.

"Good-bye, sir," she called over one shoulder, blending with the bustling crowd. Her boots resounded down the walkway, and she continued across the road, heedless of the many horses, buggies and wagons traveling there. Just as her feet touched the opposite side, a horse neighed; hoofs threatened; and someone lifted her, disrupting urgent cares.

"Are you hurt?" the man asked.

"As if you cared," she snapped, tearing from Thomas's hold and stopping his gloved hand from touching her again. Giving no thanks, she glared into his shaded eyes.

"Then I'll be on my way." Former warmth had turned passive and icy. He grasped his black stallion's reins, whipped around and sprinted off.

Why did she feel slighted from his obvious indifference? Locating profitable employment and safe residence, of more importance, she put all else aside and concentrated upon that.

Men and women paraded down Woodward Avenue. Horse driven wagons and buggies rambled across frozen ground, as Imogene sighted other shops and businesses. Eyes fell upon the only remaining dress shop in the city.

Factories produced most clothing now, but she would not consider seeking employment there. Such a job, too time-consuming, would hamper duties with the suffragette cause. And she'd sewed odd pieces for Florence before and knew the woman paid well. Perhaps flexible hours and openings were available. If not, Maude's help remained. But Imogene still felt troubled. How long could she lean upon her faithful friend?

"Imogene!" The voice came from an approaching male.

"Impossible woman!" Mr. Johnson spat.

"Sir?" she said, suspecting his last statement might have been directed at her.

"Never mind. Florence can't help the ceremony's so close." Composure enveloped his sharp features after he saw her. "My daughter's, Johnetta, wedding dress needs preparing."

Not certain he would accept, Imogene offered assistance. Her sewing skills had passed Florence's discerning eyes.

"Good," Mr. Johnson replied. "The woman did recommend you."

26

When their conversation ended, Imogene had been promised flexible hours and steady employment. She had six months to complete his daughter's marriage dress. Nuptials were scheduled July fifteenth. Elated at her good fortune, she sought rooms at Miss Annabelle's respectable boarding house on Second Avenue. She prayed rooms were available. Then thoughts of vacating her home, the place that held memories of family, sorrowed. But recalling blessings of acquired work and promised pay compensated and dispelled unfortunate happenings. And with future self-sufficiency Thomas would be out of her affairs.

***

Seth flung his coat aside. It lay upon a velvet chair, threatening to slid upon the green carpet.

"Who clawed you?"

"Stubborn, cantankerous female!" Seth paced and turned sour looks toward Frank.

"I should've known, the weaker sex." Frank shuffled the cards between his talon-like fingers. "What did our virginal Johnetta do?"

"You've named the woman furthest from my mind." Answering his companion's questioning looks, Seth explained, "Bill's daughter. What troubles she's caused since coming into my life!" Even now he found it hard erasing images of her with untamed locks, barefoot, in nightgown and, like a willful child, confronting him. Hadn't he every reason to vent rage upon her? The tall woman unsettled his peace of mind and fired feelings best kept dormant. All assistance he had offered the stubborn woman had rejected.

"Get her out your system. Bed her."

"Might as well curl up with a boa constrictor," he replied. Realizing his cohort's comment intimated he lusted after and would actually engage in sex with the woman, making himself vulnerable. He asserted, "I don't have a death wish!"

"How long has it been, Seth?" Frank taunted and poured himself another drink from the decanter near his elbow. He gulped it whole and said, "Legs spread, she's no different from any other female."

His partner's coarse remarks about ladies disturbed. Frank lumped every woman together, and he obviously felt they were made for man's pleasure. But with flawed upbringing; no father present and a mother who sold her body, Seth, as usual, pardoned his friend. Hadn't he, himself, utilized the so called weaker sex when need arose? Yes, but he respected the fairer sex. It mattered not what society termed "good" or "bad" women, he'd never belittled them. But he'd had caring parents and especially a loving mother.

Rest called; night's activities were near. Seth exited, calling, "Wake me in four hours, Frank."

"Boas squeeze their prey till dead ..."

Seth froze, turned and examined his cohort gulping another drink. Should he comment upon Frank's usual caustic remark? Why prolong unpleasantness? Seeing no reason to, he proceeded down the hall.

"Then the reptile devours its prey ... whole," Frank shouted from behind, like an omen.

***

At daylight and equipped with necessary sewing items in her valise, Imogene ventured forth. On her first day of work she pulled before a gabled house. Rushing up stone steps of the three-story residence, she promptly tapped red double doors with the ram-headed knocker.

Doors opened. "May I help you?" a smiling girl asked.

"I'm the seamstress, Imogene Washington."

The light-complexioned maid issued her into warmth, took her cape and announced the arrival.

"My dear, you must protect these fine instruments for your work." The lean mortician, absent of usual black attire, grasped her still chilled hands with his dark ones. He, attired in red ornate dressing coat, molded his stern features into a smile and guided her into the eating room.

Morning smells and brightness addressed. Ham, eggs, rolls and coffee displayed upon the sideboard tempted. She'd missed breakfast. But those sensations soon passed when food and drink were given after introductions to his family, Alma and Johnetta.

While she ate with the Johnson's, little attention stayed upon his tiny wife, Alma, who smiled persistently. But the man's off-spring, warranted much attention. The pretty girl, Johnetta, must accept her as well as her handiwork. Imogene needed this job and suspected working with his daughter would not be easy.

Second thoughts assailed. Why had she, of all persons, been chosen for involvement with her adversary's future bride? Surely she would encounter Thomas there. But this opportunity she must accept and prepare the woman child, like a lamb for slaughter—marriage to devious Seth Thomas could only be termed such. These reflections saddened and disturbed. Nothing else offered flexible hours and excellent pay. What choice had she?

In an alcove, her working space, providing privacy and abundant light, Imogene established a working relationship with Johnetta. The young girl's frequent reference to her betrothed, Seth Thomas, proved burdensome, but Imogene stayed constant and suffered quietly. It inflamed her that this young girl actually worshipped the scoundrel.

"He's thirty-one, respectable; the handsomest man I've ever met," Johnetta repeatedly heralded.

Begrudgingly, Imogene nodded agreement, acknowledging his physical attributes—her loins still ached from first seeing him adorned in the silk dressing robe. But such admission did not lessen him being her enemy or far from perfect. The silly child needed educating. No woman's worth should ever be based upon her mate's, or any man's, achievements. Females, too long man's adornment, were capable of establishing their own value. But, Imogene, only an employee, kept quiet and tended her job.

29

Past noon, Johnetta excused herself without explanation. When the girl sailed from the room in the unfinished garment, Imogene prayed the one-sleeve-missing wedding dress would not fall. Accepting momentary respite, she positioned hands at her corseted waist and stretched aching neck and shoulders. How she longed for day's end, a warm meal and night's solitude.

"Later, Johnetta, I have business with your father now," echoed outside her work area, sending shock waves through her very being. Soon his deep voice faded, causing her to give quiet gratitude.

***

Days passed. Imogene's task progressed. If not for meetings with her enemy in dark hallways and upon narrow stairs, all went well. Pondering those encounters, few but bothersome, she failed to sew a bust dart on Johnetta's garb. Wishing Thomas and memories of him would disappear, Imogene inspected the wedding gown closely. She held the dress by its dainty shoulders and compared one perfect bust with the flawed one. Quietly she laughed. Imagine influential Thomas on display with his bride adorned in costly, but flawed garment! Gloating ceased at movement and voice, causing her to hastily fix the defected garment.

"I'm here!" Johnetta exclaimed, balancing upon the stool. In stocking feet, with slender pale brown arms extended, the girl awaited her assist.

Sweeping stray hairs from her brow, Imogene carefully placed the unfinished gown over Johnetta's tidy curls.

"My coiffeur could do wonders with your hair, Imogene."

Telling herself the child meant no harm, Imogene slapped the helm of Johnetta's skirts. Its many folds seemed resistant to the attack, barely moving. And she'd secured her usually loose locks with a pink ribbon. Didn't that count for something?

"Seth!" Johnetta exclaimed, jumping from her perch and pulling the man to her level, she rained kisses over his face.

30

Such display required privacy. Seeking escape, Imogene viewed the exit. Again, as if he'd read her thoughts, Thomas moved in the way, blocking her path.

"Johnetta, another is present," he said with forced calm, unfolding the girl's arms from around his broad neck.

Imogene marveled at how his powerful hands firmly and ever so gently kept the younger woman's fragile, persistent hands at bay.

"And if she weren't here—" Johnetta pouted. She pulled from him. "You would do the usual. Nothing!"

Imogene attempted to hide shock by closing her gaping lips and staring eyes. She had witnessed something revealing between her foe and this tender child. It had surprised, the idea of a virile man not doing what all men naturally did: accept feminine favors.

"No!" Johnetta cried, stamping her tiny feet. She pulled him from exiting and urged him toward a high back chair.

With legs planted firmly upon the floor and hands fisted atop the chair's padded arms, the man, clearly agitated, sat.

Imogene labeled his actions—treating Johnetta like a child and not the woman to be his wife—as classical male bigotry. She returned to the slender girl now positioned upon the stool.

"Careful, Imogene, don't make the neckline too low. Last time you forgot to stitch a seam?" The foolish girl prattled on and on.

She prayed silently for her model's silence. Why must this silly child announce her seamstress's faults? Imogene peeked at Thomas, wondering if Johnetta had wasted efforts at keeping the man's attention or interest. Seeing his eyes, black and hawk-like, weren't on his future bride, but upon her, confirmed suspicions. And when he held her startled look, neither blinking nor pretending indifference, she felt his scrutiny of her only verified his ulterior, evil motives. That's why he'd been so accommodating, wanting her to stay in the house. But, unlike, his intended, she, no silly innocent, knew the rascal's worthlessness. Anger's flush spread over her face. He had nerve!

"Wait, Seth!" interrupted prior thoughts.

"Johnetta!" Imogene shouted. Her model had taken flight again. Only switching skirts and moving feet answered her cry. It was late; she, famished and tired. Ignoring her stomach's complaints, she tidied the room; then saw Mrs. Johnson nearby.

"My daughter's very uncooperative. Please don't resign," the woman pleaded apologetically.

"I understand," Imogene assured. "I'll return bright and early." Needing the income, she had little choice.

"Don't come back, Imogene," Johnetta cried, running past as she prepared to leave. "The wedding's off!"

Donning the cape Mrs. Johnson held for her, Imogene exited.

"Please ignore my child, Imogene. Do come back."

As Imogene smiled understanding and reassurance, Thomas appeared, dressed for leaving also. He waited patiently at the exit. Giving a hasty farewell, she boarded the buggy and rode away. Evening's chill and the lone ride home was preferable to being escorted by her enemy. Hearing hooves behind, she turned and saw Thomas, not following, but taking another path.

"Good riddance!" she exclaimed, dismissing feelings of rejection.

CHAPTER 4

"Deliver me from that woman!" Seth's voice, combative, mingled with night's cold, crystallizing into frost. With one knee he prodded his horse in an opposite direction from where Imogene had gone.

Johnetta's immaturity and willfulness hadn't caused rage or held his thoughts—Imogene's mulish ungratefulness had. Without a woman too long, he still had no desire for Johnetta's open invitations at intimacy. He saw the younger female as an obstacle and foolish promise made by others, unfairly, in his name. No, the child had not enraged. He only tolerated her. Bill's daughter had aroused dormant passions, firing his blood.

Discretion dictated he avoid Imogene and let her boil in her own juices. Why persist in offering the stubborn woman help?

He recalled stopping, for no reason, at the alcove's door. Johnetta's small form even clothed in opulence hadn't captured his attention. But Imogene's bent figure, exposing stockinged calf and black boot had excited and fueled carnal thoughts, making his heart race and palms sweat. Too long without womanly satisfaction, solely, was the cause of his unrest, he insisted.

Sensing Bill Washington had had a gambling problem, why hadn't he barred the man from his club? If he had, this torment would never have happened, and he would have not encountered Imogene's scorn. Her mistreatment of him, completely unfounded, cut to the core, causing both hurt and anger. All his assist and charity she'd rejected.

He need only rid himself of the woman by evicting her from the house or ignoring her. She had proved competent by getting work with the Johnsons—the best paid employers in town. What need had she of his help. It surely was not wanted.

His temples began throbbing. Craving rest or, better yet, womanly kinship, he, in front of the mansion, redirected his mount, Shadow. In a rowdier part of town, a house he'd not visited in months offered what would appease.

Taking back roads—they, faster and less traveled—Seth arrived at the two-story, brick house called LILLY'S PLACE. He smiled in anticipation. Laughter blared from behind closed drapes, echoing through the snow-covered streets. The house's velvet window coverings, blood-red, evoked the owner's usual scarlet attire. She, Lilly, always offered him a ready ear and, if wanted, physical relief. Some needs only women could supply.

In his eagerness Seth failed to notice a familiar buggy out front. He bounded up snow-capped steps like a youngster long denied a special treat.

"Ho!" a woman's voice cried from contact with his form.

"Pardon." He stopped, steadying her cloaked form, and tipped his bowler in deference. Looking closer—something about the stately figure drew attention—he, shocked, exclaimed, "Miss Washington!"

"I'm here on legitimate business," she said as if he there for illicit reasons. Brushing her hood aside, her sandy tresses fell free. Giving him no time to explain, in a huff, she pulled from his gripe, boarded her buggy and rode off.

"Well, it's about time, lover!"

"Need a shoulder." Seeing Lilly in her usual tight, red dress, he smiled. The woman's hefty form, filling up the portal, welcomed like her wide smile and outstretched arms promised generosity. He accepted unbridled kisses from her red lips as doors closed behind their connected shapes.

***

Hours later, Seth laid upon rumpled covers. His close-trimmed head and bare chest rested upon the great bed's ornate headboard. He hadn't been long assisting one reluctant member's departure. Craving quiet, he'd left Frank to lock up. Time spent with Lilly had left him unfilled. Restlessness weighed like a boulder around his neck; longing wouldn't quit—and not because of Lilly. She'd listened and offered physical comfort, he'd declined her carnal offers. Another woman had invaded his thoughts. She invaded his mind even now.

"What business has Miss Washington here?" he'd asked Lilly.

"Imogene." Lilly had replied "Her visits are strictly legit." After having given him teasing looks, his companion had added, "Did you think she here for selling her wares?"

"No," he'd said, lying, but glad he'd been wrong. "Why does she come?"

"About that group of women she belongs to. Some of my girls have given up the profession and joined their cause."

"Thought you'd be sleeping like a baby," a male voice said.

"What?" Seth replied, pulling from his reveries.

"I've locked up." Frank stood at the door, empty glass in one hand and cards in the other.

Nodding, Seth wanted former thoughts.

"Should take my advice." Frank began exiting and closing the bedroom door.

"What?" Interest returned to the present.

"Our—your enemy. Bill's daughter's out to get you."

"Why? I've only offered help." Disbelief surfaced.

"She's launched a campaign to destroy us—you. The woman's made much headway."

"What are you talking about?"

"Many women have, at her urgings, kept our members, their men, away. Our membership's dwindling."

"Gave it little notice," he said.

"Know your enemy. Many times that has saved our necks."

"Your're right." Seth mentally recounted some escapades they'd encountered during much younger years.

Frank's lean features twisted into its usual smirk, and a knowing look fell upon his tan-colored face. "Bill's daughter put the itch in your pants; only she—not Lilly—can take it out."

Before Seth asked Frank how he knew about his recent trip to the brothel, the slender man left, closing the door.

Light illuminated and warmth radiated over Seth's slouched form. Deep in thought, trying to sort out recent disclosures about Imogene, prevented him from sleep. Mulling over frequent absences of many previously faithful members, added credence to Frank's disclosure. How could he ignore Imogene's personal war against him? His shrinking membership and Lilly's loss girls proved Bill's daughter's persuasive powers. She was a force to face and, if need be, fight. But feeling responsible for her sad condition weighed on his heart. He should have followed his first mind and rejected Bill from the club.

Light broke through opened drapes. A new day had arrived. Gaining control over guilt, anger mounted, turning dangerous. He donned yesterday's clothing, exited his room and entered the hall. Slipping pass Frank's opened door, he glanced at his friend's clothed form sprawled across the huge bed—his partner always slept thus. This practice had benefited both of them often during their younger, wayward years.

"Where're you going?"

"Bill's daughter!" he responded, neither softening inflamed tones nor slowing hurried pace.

"Use her well," Frank leered. "Be done with the hellcat!"

Having neither time nor patience to explain his visit with Imogene would not involve sexual intimacy, Seth snatched his outerwear from where he'd thrown it earlier and exited, slamming the door. Morning's freeze, not lessening his anger only fueled it. Increased heartbeat, distended nostrils and sweaty palms indicated he literally simmered while prodding his horse toward Hague Street.

After several loud knocks, she didn't answer—reminiscent of the first time. Drawn curtains, transparent, didn't hide the view. Inside, furniture still stood, certainly indicated she'd not moved. At this hour, where was the woman?

Standing in the chill, his fuse cooled. Bathed, freshly clothed and breakfasted, he best confront her. Better for him to go home and see her later.

***

Deep in concentration, Imogene studied the white wedding gown, hanging upon it's wire form. Relieved she didn't need the girl now—Johnetta's restlessness and constant chatter grated so—pray the outfit's completion wouldn't be long. Odd sewing for the Johnsons would still give good income, and she had more time for her first calling and only love, suffragetism.

Bending to inspect the gown's wide border, the airy fabric skimmed down her arms, caressing, it seemed, fine hairs upon her skin's surface. The sensation conjured things untried: intimacy between man and woman. Feeling aftermath of such thoughts, she inhaled, thrusting her proud bosom forward. While engaged, an unknown presence drew. Turning, her lips gaped in speechless surprise.

He, the cause of her distress, barred the exit. Dressed differently than his usual knickers and lace shoes, Seth Thomas, in black boots, stood wide-legged. Checked trousers and black lounge coat, complimented his flawless physique.

"Johnetta's not here," she said, hoping to hasten his departure and ease her mounting discomfort.

"I know. She's on an outing with Mrs. Johnson."

"Surely, your business is not with me!" She cried while forcing herself not to retreat from his approach.

"You're mistaken, Imo—Miss Washington, it is."

Realizing he had nearly used her given name, denoting, she believed, his superior position, bravery surged, and she glared into black eyes—that held hers as intently. For the first time, she saw his orbs weren't black, but were the exact hue of his dark brown coloring. The perfect match gave him an intense look that penetrated her core, making her sway.

As if in no hurry, he unbuttoned his coat, displaying a a trim, waistcoated middle. Keeping her regard, he moved closer.

"Yes?" she forced out, stilling herself and praying he would state his mission and leave.

"I went to your home earlier. You weren't there." He looked at her as if for explanation.

"So?" She felt no obligation in giving excuse for not being available for his convenience.

"My offer still stands. You need not vacate the house."

She knew it! How dare he play upon her misfortune? Did he think her, like his future bride, obsessed with him? Well, she, no silly child, wasn't blind to his evil intentions.

"I want nothing from you, sir." Enveloped in the man's essence—he seeped maleness—she fought at yielding. "I'll suffer homelessness before I accept anything from you!"

"It may come to that," His tone didn't sound triumphant. One gold earring, in his ear, glistened as his head turned, drawing attention to the troubling expression upon his beardless face. "Have I given you, Miss Washington, cause for fight? Your efforts will harm, not only me, but two other innocents. I'm their sole provider."

Innocents? Children? How could she have known. Wanting no blame for injuring his off-spring, she resolved to cease this personal battle.

Offering no explanation or verification, he glared at her with unmistakable rage in his crescent-shaped eyes.

"Sorry," she whispered, looking away. "I never imagined or meant harm—"

"Don't play innocent with me! Your underhanded schemes were fully intentional."

"If I had known about your children—"

"Seth!" interrupted her words.

"Later, Johnetta," Seth said, redirecting the speaker toward the exit.

"Only if you promise," Johnetta demanded.

Keeping Imogene in view, Seth nodded at his betrothed.

"Don't make me wait long." The child reluctantly left, not closing the door.

"Then the war's over." Relief blanketed his handsome face.

"I can't harm children, even yours," she admitted.

"I have no children." He shot her puzzling looks.

Clearly hearing his admission, she felt he'd mislead on purpose. Angry, not wanting further explanation, her sentiments reverted. How stupid to forget he, the enemy, wouldn't use any trick at getting his way.

"Friends?" He presented an ungloved hand in truce.

"Never!" she cried, rejecting any verbal or physical offer. "You're deceitful and make your living from vice."

"That's your opinion. Show me what law says operating a gentlemen's club is illegal?"

Father gave up his property and died there," she countered.

"You blame me for his death?" No longer harsh, his tone softened. "You can have the house." He gathered her in his arms.

Wrapped in warmth by his touch, she felt secure, forgetting he was the enemy. Resting and releasing all dispute, she felt heaven must be this.

"Let me help you. Bill, your father—"

"No!" she cried, pulling away. Father's name had awakened the reasons for her vendetta. "I neither want nor need you!"

"I'm sorry, Imogene, you feel this way." He maintained the physical distance she'd created, but his eyes seemed intent upon bridging the void.

"Seth!" Johnetta had entered and pulled at his sleeve like a jealous brat seeking attention. "You've stayed with my seamstress long enough." She gave Imogene a haughty look. And when Seth still hesitated, the silly girl protruded her full bottom lip. "You neglect me terribly."

Reluctantly turning away, he followed his intended.

Now alone, Imogene tore from Seth's lingering presence. Still experiencing his warmth, her senses felt gorged, drowning in the man's masculinity. She must leave and see to more urgent matters. After securing hooded cape, she bade quick farewells and hurried past the front parlor—Seth's deep voice and Johnetta's childish laughter came from there. Outside, boarding her buggy, Imogene insisted she was glad to be free of the rogue. Then why did a sense of loss still assail?

Sweeping such disquiet away, Imogene ventured home, she'd acquired rooms at Miss Gertrude Turner's boarding house. Clothes and keepsakes required packing. Larger items, she had no room or use for. Let Thomas do what he wanted with them along with the house.

Amongst tears, embraces and expressions of gratitude, she informed Maude and her parents of new residence—only a few streets away. Now one major duty awaited. A task she both savored and dreaded. Midnight's late hour did not deter because activity still functioned at her destination. Pulling before the mansion, she jumped from the buggy onto the cold, hard ground and raced to the entrance.

Light peeked from behind drapes, partly opened. The portal sprung wide before she knocked. An elderly man, Imogene could not recognize, bumped into her. He tipped his lowered, hatted head, apologized and hurried away. But she knew the slender, hatted male at the entrance. Thomas's friend, Frank Kossel, did not step aside for her entry. He displayed usual contempt.

"Someone there, Frank?"

Not awaiting any response, Imogene swept past Frank's moving form. She came face to face with her enemy, Seth Thomas.

He stood in what he'd worn earlier except for daycoat and neckcloth, but, none the less, looking resplendent. His white, unbuttoned shirt looked immaculate against the dark hue of his broad neck and chest.

"I'm giving notice." She dangled keys like a hunter would wave bait before its prey, ready for the kill. Smiles played upon her lips. "Do what you want with the house, Mr. Thomas. I no longer reside there."

When he finally extended a hand, she dropped the keys in his cupped palm and turned toward the exit. Frank stepped aside, swinging the portal wide for her hasty departure. Footfalls sounded behind. Only after boarding the buggy and glancing back, had she known those footsteps where her enemy's, Seth Thomas.

He stood in the open, upon the porch, with one black riding boot perched upon a perron. Cold winds fluttered the opened collar beneath his glaring face, and one hand laid, clenched, at his side.

Feeling the cold bite against her exposed teeth, she cared not. Triumphant expression stayed upon her lips. Smiling wide, she rambled away.

CHAPTER 5

"You seen him lately?"

"Not since I gave him the keys to my—the property, Maude." Dismissing concern clouding her friend's features, Imogene continued. "Good riddance!"

"He's powerful, Immie, from an established family. He could harm you. What if you required his help?"

"Never!" she replied. "Not in a million years will I accept anything from him."

"Don't burn your bridges," Maude cautioned. "What if our fight for women's rights hinged upon his assist?"

"There're others—Mr. Johnson came to mind—as powerful we can call on." She donned her outerwear.

"Never say never." Maude followed her to the front exit.

Ignoring her companion's warnings, Imogene departed after a hasty embrace. And while headed toward her new residence, she recalled an occurrence of two weeks ago that had irritated. But before the event fully registered, a presence and voice interrupted.

"Good morning, Miss Washington."

"Oh!" she cried, startled and hastening her horse.

"I won't take much of your time," Seth Thomas said, effortlessly matching her quickened pace. "Where's Frank?"

Stopping abruptly, her horse neighed from pull upon the animal's reins. She faced Thomas. "Frank's not my ward. He's yours," she spewed in opposite contrast to his civil tones.

"You were with him last," Thomas said too assuredly.

How could he know of the encounter with Frank?

"You and he argued outside the Eastside Eatery two weeks ago." Again, he'd answered her silent query.

Her lips opened in amazement, but sound didn't come.

"He's been missing since then. Frank always tells me of his whereabouts, that is, unless he's been greatly vexed."

"Any anguish your friend's been caused has not come from me!" She turned and rode away, trying to erase her opponent's harsh shouts.

"Your underhanded tactics against me have proved you would not help." His voice faded as she gained distance.

***

"Good! I've finished Johnetta's wedding dress," Imogene sighed, putting aside memories of her and Seth's last meeting. She approached Maude's seated form. "I'm willing and able."

"I love your eagerness, Immie." Her friend rose, saying, "We'll go see the professor now." Maude rose from her seat.

Imogene followed eagerly. At last, arrangements were made for studies in elocution to further her abilities as speaker for suffragettism. Venturing forth near Maude's side, gusting winds fluttered their skirts and capes, but never deterred their steps.

"We'll walk, Immie. It's not far."

Like a well-trained solder she by-passed her buggy and walked with her ally down barren, tree-lined Second Avenue. Seven houses away they climbed stone steps and knocked upon double French doors.

"You're expected, Miss Graves and companion," the male servant said and directed them to warm quarters.

"Sit here," Maude said as she cleared away papers and books from a lumpy divan. "He's so messy," she added.

"Isn't that a sign of genius?" Imogene half-teased as she sunk into flowered cushions and adjusted her form accordingly while scanning parchments scattered across carpet and desk.

"Dearest Maude," a bespectacled male said, entering.

"Hiram!" Maude replied in a formal manner.

Imogene saw them approach and touch—him holding Maude's dark hands between his pale fingers. Their manners appeared too stiff, her ally and the elderly man's eyes spoke volumes, making Imogene feel intrusive. She suspected this man was, or had been Maude's lover. But her friend had never spoke of such personal matters. Imogene only knew she felt out of place.

"This is my prize pupil, Miss Imogene Washington," Maude finally said.

"Miss Washington, delighted." Relinquishing Maude's hand, he grasped Imogene's, saying, "Cold hands. Warm heart."

Imogene smiled kindly. She knew her heart had nothing to do with her hands, chilled because she'd not worn gloves in inclement weather. But attracted to his fatherly, still attractive appeal, she welcomed the learned man's tutelage.

"Dearest Maude has assured me you are fertile soil, ready at taking the giant step for women. You realize, once endowed with these powers, much will be required of you?"

"Of course!" she exclaimed in spite of Maude's anxious looks. Dismissing all worries, she locked them away. Whatever confronted, beast or man, she would rise and conquer.

A week gave them little time before Professor Anderson's departure. Instructions, intense and thorough, began that same day and continued well after midnight, making it mandatory she spend the entire week at her mentor's residence. Forget proper society's rules. All for the "cause" was her motto.

Instructions started with him critiquing a twenty minuet speech she'd given recently. It involved a talk given to a group of women at the brothel. The oration urged women to fight for independence from man's self-serving rule. In the animated and fiery sermon against male superiority, Imogene feared she'd forgotten herself and might have offended Professor Anderson, he of that species. But his approving smile and nod dispelled those fears. And When she finished, his words solidified the impression.

Excellent, my dear!" An amused smile accompanied his next comment. "We men do yield more physical prowess, but the fairer sex, I have found, are aptly endowed in other ways." Then he turned more serious, "Let's work on projection and body language. Refining these qualities will enhance what you already possess. Perfection's the goal."

Hours later, after dark, Imogene went to appointed rooms she and Maude would share. Quickly disrobing for bed at her companion's urging, she donned a frilly sleeping gown offered by Maude. Not expressing wonder why Professor Hiram Anderson owned feminine attire, she, nonetheless, shot Maude questioning looks.

"They're mines," her ally laughed freely. Not giving explanation, she exited with, "Sleep tight, Immie."

Alone at last, her eyes searched the surroundings. White lace and pink frills indicated the room belonged to no man, or, at least, not a manly man. As she reclined upon cool sheets and soft mattress, a knowing smile fell on her lips—Professor was Maude's lover. And as Imogene drifted into sleep, another male, Thomas, seeped into her dreams, making slumber uneasy.

Awakening, she glared into brightness coming from opened drapes. It seemed she'd not slept—her and Seth's last confrontation regarding Frank had grated all night. What made him think she knew of Frank's whereabouts? Yes, she and his ally had argued outside the eatery due to the man's monetary offer in exchange for one sexual favor, not for himself, but for his boss, Seth Thomas. Wondering if the rogue, Thomas, had put his partner of to the offer, she whispered, "Of course, he did. The nerve!"

"You up, Immie," shattered her reflections.

"Yes. I'll be ready in no time." Springing from the bed's comfort, she washed, dressed quickly and hurried to breakfast and studies.

As days passed, she saw things going her way. Soon she would solicit funds and laud, like Susan B Anthony and Sojourner Truth, for the women's movement. And reliable sources told her Thomas's membership had lessened by thirds and her former house had remained empty, in disrepair. Even matters concerning his partner, Frank, had caused no further repercussions for her. If only her foe's magnificent image would cease invading her dreams.

The man's essence had filled sleeping hours. His allure compelled and even when awakened, she felt great emptiness, a gnawing desire, like a person chilled to the bone and needing warmth. No other man had ever had such hold or power over her.

"The week's over, Immie," Maude exclaimed. "Hiram's told you of tonight's event?"

"Yes, I'm willing and ready," Imogene asserted.

"I hope so." Maude's voice sounded doubtful.

"I would face the very devil or Seth Thomas for our cause.

"Many women should be so lucky." Why did Maude seem amused?

"I don't understand." Perplexed by her ally's statement and humor, Imogene slid forward in her seat to listen intently.

"You will," Maude sighed as her small bosom deflated.

Chills of apprehension cursed through Imogene's body.

"There will be many influential persons at this affair tonight." Maude paused after each word, as if, giving her time to absorb their implications. "It's really a celebration for Hiram. But he feels this is a good opportunity for you to offer appeal to the prominent and wealthy men attending.

A confident smile widen her lips as her head nodded. She certainly had no fear approaching any man or group for funds, sponsorship or whatever for "the cause". So why had worry still clouded her friend's face?

Maude rose. Her lips opened. She appeared engrossed.

"I'll leave now and get ready." Imogene stood.

"No, Everything's here for you." Maude directed her into a dressing room. 'We can't have you wearing anything but the finest for this grand occasion."

She took no offense at her companion's remarks. The only clothing she owned were outdated and dull-colored, none right for a grand affair. So like an obedient student, she hastened her toilet and dressing.

"Life is a challenge, Immie," Maude commented while assisting and directing preparations.

Imogene nodded while disrobing.

"Things must be done for our great cause," Maude said, hurrying her into the awaiting bath water.

Climbing into the claw footed tub and easing into soapy, still warm waters, Imogene had little time to enjoy comfort and quiet before Maude reappeared.

"This opportunity will give you exposure and might cause great hardship."

"You act as if I'm to be sacrificed." Imogene halted activity and studied her companion's somber expression.

"It may come to that." Maude quickly added, "But it'll depend upon your point of view."

"I don't understand."

"You will." Maude disappeared, but soon returned. "Come. My hairdresser's waiting."

"Hairdresser?"

"How many times have you told me, Immie, you can't do a thing with your hair?"

Maude disappeared before she could expound. This whole assignment involved much mystery. Why did worry stay, plastered across her ally's proud features? But trusting the older woman, she resolved to accept and do whatever had been asked. And if woman's worth depended upon her success or failure, could she not give her best?

***

"Very appealing, dear. You're the picture of correctness and beauty!" Professor Anderson exclaimed as he accompanied Imogene in a Hansom Cab.

She blushed at his compliments and admired his proud figure decked out in finery of black trousers, cutaway and checkered greatcoat. Before she could compliment the elder man, he grasped her silk gloved hands.

"No one will deny you this evening, my dear." His lips widened, seeming to disappear into his bushy mustache and silver sideburns. "You will triumph."

She beamed and patted the professor's coat sleeve in appreciation of his praise, encouragement and instruction. How could she not succeed with such positive reinforcements? Like a well-trained soldier, she mentally reviewed the high points of her speech. No one had told her where the celebration would take place. She only knew it was at a prominent house. And at this affair she must address wealthy men—she knew not how many nor their names. The goal being petition of funds for suffragettism.

The cab rambled over frozen ground. Blustering winds beat against their padded enclosure. She wiggled her stockinged toes. Elbow-length gloves, encased normally chilly, bare hands and matched her velvet slippers and emerald gown. She felt indulgent warmth. No need existed to hug herself, but she did. Maude's costly sable—on loan—wrapped her body in softness, luxuriousness and warmth. No one felt more pampered or priviledged than she.

They stopped behind numerous parked vehicles. Accepting Professor's assist by placing a gloved hand upon his forearm, excitement swept over her. They paraded up red carpeted stairs with others and beneath red banners, hanging from the home's balcony. Voices and music greeted as double doors opened. They stepped in a marbled hall, and formally dressed male, his face shrouded in shadows, took outerwear and directed them to the massive ballroom. Something about her surroundings ... Had she been here before?

Glowing chandeliers softly illuminated elegantly dressed persons clustered in small groups, and string instruments lent an air of heavenliness to the large room, adverting attention. Something else compelled. She glanced over one bare shoulder.

A dark gentlemen stood near an adjoining entrance. His splendid form demanded notice. She would not look away. How distinguished he appeared in black cutaway, trousers, white shirt and neckcloth, so stark in coloring against his ebony skin. What glittered near one ear? Glaring, she nearly screamed. It couldn't be! But it was. She'd entered the bowels of hell, and the devil himself stood at its portals, Seth Thomas.

Feeling betrayed and angry, she now knew the reasons for Maude's constant worried demeanor. Why hadn't her friend said something? Recalling how she'd swore to face Lucifer, himself, for their cause, anger soon dissipated. Once again, she vowed to succeed. Tearing her gaze from the man, she observed some elder women occupying padded benches and fanning themselves. Groups of older men glanced about, as if, seeking diversion. Four young men and women coupled off and gathered in quieter, dimmer, more secluded areas.

"Imogene, my dear ..."

She looked up and welcomed the professor's hand.

"Come. Our host desires your presence."

Bracing herself, she expected him to approach Seth Thomas, believing he the host. But Professor led her elsewhere.

Welcoming her escort's firm support, she pranced across marble flooring until they stood before an elderly gentleman.

"This is the young lady, Miss Imogene Washington, you were asking about, Ben," Professor Anderson said.

"Miss Washington, is it?" the old gentleman, introduced as Mr. Benjamin Thomas, said.

When he did not stand, she thought he was an invalid. The chair's ornate woodwork and plush high back had hidden its actual use. She bent to his level and extended a hand. Two huge wheels on either side of his seat and cushioned foot rest confirmed her assumption.

I've heard so much about you," the elder Thomas said as he grasped her hand between his veined, slightly quivering ones. "My grandson has spoken of you."

Unease assailed when she turned where Ben Thomas indicated. But the man's hand, similar to her light coloring, offered warmth and, somehow, support. Strength's revival made her stand even taller, beholding her adversity's familiar scrutiny.

"Miss Washington," Seth Thomas said with cold formality, bordering upon indifference. His hands, not lifting in welcome, stayed at his side. The bitterness in his eyes matched the frown upon his sensual lips.

She slipped her hands from between the old gentleman's and coolly nodded acknowledgment to Seth. Inspecting both men again, she saw the likeness between the elder's sallow-hued face and the younger man's sepia features. Both displayed proud handsomeness.

"You're Bill's daughter," Ben Thomas recaptured her hand and held on. "I only met your father on one occasion. But his association with the Graves, our dear friends, makes him and you our friends as well.

Returning the old man's broad smile and accepting his favor, she wondered how his grandson, the scoundrel, issued from such fine stock. Ben Thomas had won her heart. His faithful confidant she would always be.

"If there's anything—costs do not matter—let me know. I will promptly comply," Ben added.

"I appreciate your regard and offer," she proclaimed. But, quietly, she declared never would she accept or ask anything from his grandson. And as her eyes turned from Seth's cold perusal of her, they fell upon foods readied for this event.

Forgotten to eat in her hurried readying for this event, Imogene's gaze fixed upon the abundant fare displayed on three sideboards. Colorful cuisine tempted and teased. Her stomach flipped. Dizziness beset. She wavered, seeking some foundation.

"Are you ill, Imogene dear?" Professor Anderson captured her thrusting hands.

"I ..." she heard herself whisper before the room began revolving, becoming one encompassing rotation. Hands slipped about her body, like some great force, drawing her close to maleness and well-remembered heat and essence as she slipped into oblivion.

CHAPTER 6

Hints of sound intruded in the black room's silence. Light like colored ribbons eased into view, exploding its reflective hue and shadows upon gold bedcovers. Illumination stopped at one cylinder-shaped bedpost that reached to a ceiling splattered with naked, curly-headed cherubs.

Shaving lotion, tobacco and brandy, manly scents, floated in the air. Imogene's nose twitched. Her eyelids fluttered. Brightness beckoned her further from slumber. With difficulty she raised from comfort and warmth.

"I didn't intend to disturb you."

Imogene's eyes popped opened and fixed upon silhouette, blocking the room's exit. Her hands grasped rumpled covers and jerked their softness close to her flannel-covered bosom. She held them beneath her chin. In spite of opened lips, she spoke nothing.

"I'll just leave this."—The man's hand held an object.

Recognizing Seth Thomas as the man holding the offending receptacle, she recoiled. Chamber pots were no longer in use since bathrooms were inside now and equipped with more modern arrangements and especially in a place like the Thomas Mansion. Though painted with daisies, why did he still own the old thing?

"There's indoor bath and toilet." He indicated an adjacent room. "This was a necessity." He slid the pot under the bed. "You could keep nothing down. It's handy on certain occasions."

She blushed to think of herself being in such an unbecoming position, spewing her stomach's contents on everything. Might she have dislodged some of that matter on him, her enemy? She felt little recompense for it would have put her at great disadvantage, appearing helpless and weak. Thomas must never perceive her as not fully in control.

Out of curiosity, she inspected him, and saw he no longer wore formal clothes. Examining lawn shirt, partly opened at the neck, and a tan waistcoat, she wondered if earlier attire had been soiled and that was why he'd redressed. Alone in his presence, she suddenly felt exposed and turned attention to surroundings.

The massive place, decorated in bronze, gold and mahogany indicated it must be a man's room. She dismissed the idea that these personal quarters were her enemy's. Imogene's eyes swept over the chamber's ponderous furnishings: wardrobe, chairs, secretary and books, lining an entire wall. Gold velvet drapes covered ceiling-high windows. Then she noticed her aqua-colored evening dress spread across a gold brocaded divan—a place, she had heard, used often for a quick tryst. When her gaze fell upon aqua slippers, silk stockings and crumpled underclothes, former uneasiness returned, even more so. Had he undressed her?

"Ola unclothed you, Miss Washington."

His reply to her silent question caused both relief—that he had not disrobed her—and unease. How could he correctly respond to so many of her silent queries?

"Why am I here?" she uttered.

"You became ill at Professor Anderson's celebration." He continued standing over her.

"How long have I been here?" She gave him little chance at responding, "I—I must leave."

"I can't allow that, Miss Washington."

His authoritative tone made her feel at a disadvantage, him towering over her bedded form. Hopping for some advantage by getting closer to his upright position, she raised higher, keeping covers close. But there hadn't been need for that. He eased his body down to her plane and positioned upon one thigh. Their eyes met and held.

"You can't leave, Miss Washington. I apologize for my intrusion. Dr. Cook insisted I watch you closely until his follow up visit. Ola's busy with Grandfather; I could not, in good conscience, leave you unattended."

Unable to pull attention from his well-chiseled face, she observed his coarse hair, jet-black and close-trimmed. Crescent eyes indicated distant Asian ancestry, perhaps, and his generous lips seemed to smile sensuously. Those individual features fit too well together. Her eyelids fluttered, threatening closure from his intense, unnerving gaze. But sheer force of will held his black eyes until they begun traveling the width and breath of her features. She felt powerless and feared she might succumb, fainting away.

Their spirits had touched, as surely as a physical caress with breaths and lips blending.

"Ola should be free." He stood, unhinging the spell. "I'll send her to attend you."

Cool breeze from his leaving sent chills through Imogene; she wrapped her arms around her shivering body. The rain's steady, persistent pelting upon the window felt soothing and, at the same time, troubling. She fell back into the pillows.

Ola soon plowed into the room after one knock. The woman thrust a tray at Imogene, flinging its red checkered covering aside. Steam and tempting smells filled the room and Imogene's nostrils. She beheld a gold-edged bowl with chicken, rice and carrots floating in thick, yellow liquid.

"Eat slow, girl. Don't want that chamber pot full again."

Bitting into chicken, rice and carrots, Imogene chewed fiercely, watching the older woman's departing, waddling gait.

Winds howled outside, indicating the weather had turned angry and black, not unlike her mood. Imogene threw food aside, in spite of continuing hunger, and stood. She must leave this place. Minutes after standing, she knew, it'd been a mistake. The room rotated, swirling. Nothing, not grasping any stable object or easing down to the bed, could help. Eyes shut as her world rotated round and round ... falling.

***

In the same seat she'd occupied two evenings ago, Seth rested, staring into the cold hearth. In this ballroom he'd first noticed Imogene Washington. Not so much because she'd looked very different with thick hair in shinny ringlets and dressed in costly attire. But something else, surely, had drawn him. He couldn't say what exactly. When their eyes had met while he had stood at another, seldom used entrance, a great force had summoned, making him study the beguiling creature dressed in shoulder bearing, aqua gown and elbow length gloves.

The woman's fiery hazel eyes; the turn of thick, sandy hair bouncing about her swanlike neck and across her naked shoulders, perhaps, had awakened recognition.

"Ben's waiting."

Seth turned toward Ola and smiled acknowledgment. He stood, ready at performing customary duties of spending time with his grandparent before bedtime.

"Did you check on Miss Washington?" He masked over concern with an indifferent tone. But Ola's frown indicated he'd failed. Hadn't she warned him of "the girl's" ploys against them?

"I left food with the girl," the elder woman said with bitterness, walking away. "She ain't got no business here. It's like fooling with a snake."

Why did Ola's reference to a viper upset? Hadn't he made a similar implication?

"I'll attend grandfather," he said. "Then I'll see to her."

"Ain't right!" Ola moaned, leaving. "The girl here!"

Having tucked Grandfather in bed, they talked over two hours of former and current memories. And when Ben yawned and closed his wrinkled eyes, Seth stood and tipped toward the exit.

"How's Bill's brat?"

Seth stopped in the hall, remembering his next task.

"I'm speaking of—"

"Yes," he said, irritated with Frank's reference. "Do you know her well enough to call her Bill's brat?" Not wanting any response, Seth left. How long had Imogene been unattended?

Ola rushed pass, folded linen in her arms.

"Did you check on her yet?" he asked, stopping.

"That's your duty!"

Seth sprinted down the carpeted hallway and rapped at the entrance of his usual chambers. Prompt response didn't come. He pushed the ajar door fully opened and looked inside. Covers were displaced. His bed was empty. Had she gone? Discounting hurt feelings, he whispered, "Good riddance! Ungrateful woman!"

"Ohhh ..."

Moaning caught his attention. He searched from where the sound had come. Unable to locate its source, he entered the room further and discerned a white form, crumpled at the foot of the bed, causing him to rush over and bend at the fallen figure upon the black carpet.

Imogene laid there. Her already sallow coloring, even more so, almost blended with her sandy-colored lashes. Freckles appeared more pronounced scattered across her medium wide nose. Usually pink lips were parted and too pale, but still alluring.

"Imogene," he whispered, gently touching, checking to see if she'd broken or injured anything.

"Dizzy," he heard her mumble.

"You must have fallen. Are you hurt? Anything broken?" he asked. "Why didn't you call?"

"Don't think so." Pulling from him, she hugged the bedpost. "Don't need help!"

"Let me just ..." He reached for her.

"No!" she cried, if, somewhat, weakly.

Stubborn woman! he almost shouted, before deciding to leave her to her own defenses. But he stayed close in case she might stumble. Balancing upon one knee, he watched, with reluctant admiration, her determined, valiant attempts at standing. After several of her futile tries, he lifted, ignoring her loud objections, and deposited her upon the bed.

"Didn't need help!" She snatched covers up, holding them close, and shot him stabbing looks.

"We all need help sometimes." He'd nearly laughed at her wilful antics—strange, such behavior always irritated when done by Johnetta. But now he only smiled indulgently, amused.

"Well—" She appeared flustered, then said assuredly, "In any case, I didn't want your assist." Eyes fluttered close as she sunk into the pillows, closing her eyes.

"Frank, Ola, get the doctor!" he summoned, dismissing mounting wounded feelings caused by his ungrateful guest.

"What's wrong? Frank's gone for Dr Cook." Ola stood at the room's entrance. Her brownish features furrowed in concern.

"She's fainted." His hand brushed over Imogene's forehead and across one cheek. "She feels cold."

"Well, put more cover on the girl. Here." Ola thrusted a flowered coverlet in his arms. "Frank should return soon. The elder woman left.

Returning to his disabled charge, he observed her features, appealing by any standards. They were even more comely in quiet, devoid of their usual scrowl. And her recumbrant form conjured memories of softness pressing against, into his body as he had lifted her. Awaiting the doctor, he, dismissing decorum— they were neither engaged nor wed—perched upon the bed.

Surveying accustomed quarters, his bedroom, nothing ... and everything ... had changed. Imogene made the difference. Upon the leather setee her clothing laid: delicate underthings, emerald gown, matching slippers and moulded corset. Adverting his eyes, they fell upon white, almost transparent things. When he recognized the appearel as stockings, deep stirrings grew inside. Too long he'd been without a woman. And they were ready and available. Lillian, Johnetta—who constantly threw herself at him—and others, more than eager, would supply carnal needs.

"Doc's here," Frank said, rushing inside and disrupting Seth's reveries.

"Get Ola! Need a woman in attendance." Dr. Cook nearly knocked Frank and Seth over as he hastened toward Imogene. Covers were thrown aside for greater access to the patient.

Feeling displaced, Seth backed away, easing from the room. He took Frank with him as Ola came huffing down the hall

"Girl's more trouble than she's worth!" the elder woman said, scurrying past.

"Ola needs help," Seth mumbled, once again realizing his aunt; especially since Imogene's confinement, worked too hard for one of her elder age.

"She does good for a sixty year old," Frank replied. "When widowed, didn't she agree to move in only upon earning her keep and not accepting your charity?"

Seth nodded, remembering his aunt called upon two girls for hire at her discretion. He trailed Frank into the gaming area. One member, Mr. Potts, remained at this late hour.

"How's Miss Imogene?" the storekeeper asked.

Seth studied the old man's face which showed much concern and wondered if the oldster had personal dealings with his sick guest. Shaking off questions that didn't involve him, Seth turned away, not responding.

"Don't know," Frank replied in his stead. "Doc's still with her."

"She's mulish," Mr. Potts remarked, regret written over his whiskered features.

Truer words were never spoken, Seth thought.

"Be easier if she married."

Again, Seth silently concurred with the senior.

"No man'll have her," Frank sneered.

"Not true!" Mr. Potts declared. "I asked for her hand." The man's slight chest puffed up like a strolling rooster.

"You what?" Seth asked, after shock ebbed from the old buzzard's claim. He couldn't see tall, feisty Imogene Washington and enfeebled Mr. Potts connected, not in any manner.

"Tried courtin' her many times. She always turned me down." The elder scratched his gray head and added most sincerely, "Can't understand why."

Seth almost echoed Frank's snort, but he kept a straight face and stayed silent. What business of his was it if intimacy existed between the disabled woman in his bed and Mr. Potts?"

"Best leave." The storeowner followed Frank to the exit.

Seth paced. His thoughts, likewise, swayed back and forth over the creature inhabiting his rooms; disrupting his life; making him consider endangering Grandfather, Ola's and his own livelihood. Even now he still felt her womanliness mold with his body; arousing desires, needs, too long unfulfilled.

"Seth," Dr. Cook said. "Miss Washington appears not to have broken anything. She has some bruises from the fall, but that'll heal. Gave her a sedative. She's quite headstrong."

"Yes," he affirmed. "More than called for."

"Seems you two have butted heads a few times," Dr. Cook teased.

"That's not the half of it." He reached for a decanter of whiskey. "Would you like a drink?"

"Not while I'm working." The grinning physician checked his timepiece. "Left the wife abed with a promise I hurry back." A sly smile spread across his brown face. "Emma, my wife, don't take no foolishness. Strong woman. Much like your guest Miss Washington." He donned outerwear and with anticipation upon his lips, he departed, saying, "A woman like that keeps fires burning in a man."

Seth had little chance confirming the doctor's words.

"Doc say when she might leave?" Frank had returned.

"He gave her a sleeping potion. In the morning, perhaps, if she's improved."

"Well, not tonight," Frank snarled.

"You never did tell me what happened between you two in front of the eatery." His partner's blatant eagerness for their sick guest's departure bothered. Still holding the decanter, he poured himself a drink. When no response came, he faced Frank. "She denied any relationship, not even a slight friendship."

"You care?" Frank reached for the untouched drink in Seth's hand.

"Be my guest," he said, releasing the goblet. Watching his ally down the whiskey in one gulp, opened more questions. Frank, always cool and collected, seemed disturbed. Why?

"Whatever your professed enemy admitted, was a lie!"

"She didn't really tell me anything. I'm wondering what occurred between you two—something monumental, personal— to have caused a public argument in front of the busiest eatery in town and made you not inform me. We've always kept each other advised."

Usual glibness seemed to have escaped Frank. Troubling looks swept across his lean face as he looked away. But when they, once again observed Seth, customary assuredness had returned. "Does it matter?"

"We have a partnership. Nothing must come between that."

"Believe me, friend, I'll never let any woman, certainly not that ungrateful—"

Seth, unsure why his ally omitted the unkind label intended for Imogene, decided to forget the query and the man's offenses.

"I don't won't her!" Frank bellowed. "My women must be easy and more than ready."

Seth nodded. Experience verified his partner spoke truth. In their long association, Frank had always favored and bedded the excessively willing, brimming with sweetness, women. Too much "sugar"—in foods and females—always sickened Seth.

"She's in the perfect place," Frank ribbed. "Your bed."

Not responding, Seth threw the man cutting looks and stood. Exiting, he said, "Must attend our ill guest."

"Believe me, friend, there's never been anything physical between her and me." His voice brimmed with sincerity. "Just don't trust her. What happened at the eatery only confirmes rumors. She has wagged war on us and is near succeeding."

The club's diminishing membership confirmed Frank's words.

"Should counterattack. You have her in your bed—"

"No comment," he rasped, having little patience for his comrade's implication that he lusted after the damsel upstairs. "I'll help you close up after checking Miss Washington."

"Don't rush. Taming her'll take time, maybe all night."

Ignoring the man's insinuation, Seth left and ventured upstairs. After tapping upon the door and no response came, he remembered Dr. Cook had administered a sleeping balm. If she rested, why enter? But he'd not forgotten Imogene's earlier mishap. After knocking again, he eased the door opened. The chambers emitted manly scents, his, and Imogene's own womanly essences which, to him, evoked honeyed, sultry smells. Tangled bedcovers barely revealed sandy-hued curls. The ringlets lay riotously about her face.

How angelic her features looked at rest. Her face's symmetry, even more appealing, evoked self-same cravings deep in his loins. Never would he follow Frank's counsel and seduce her. She must take the lead. Impossible! It would never happen. The woman hated his guts. Watching her in such a compromising position, he started to leave.

"Father," she mumbled. "Why?" A moan escaped. "So alone."

Baseless guilt resurged from within. If only he had banned Bill ... Mentally he shook off unwarranted blame. He recalled all kindness offered and ready assistance given the old man and his daughter. Bill's home, needing much repair before rental occupation, would cost more than the domicile's actual value.

Heeding better judgment, Seth touched the sleeping woman's cheek. Like summer's heat, moist and hot, her breath misted his flesh, reawakening cravings best kept imprisoned.

"Stop!" she cried, beating his hand. "Get away!"

"It's me, Imo—," he whispered, grasping her fists. "Only making certain you've no fever."

Stilling, she unhinged sandy-colored lashes. Hazel orbs stared, searching his. Her lips parted, making no sound. She separated fully from his touch and sat up, letting covers fall.

He felt need for apology and said, "Sorry for intruding, but I needed to know you hadn't had another fall."

"I must leave this place!" Her hazel eyes glared at him, clearly daring him to refute her assertion.

When she stood, abandoning the covers, he only watched, saying nothing. And as she searched the room, wayward locks enticed. He suspected she looked this way after lovemaking. He gazed upon her night-clothed body. The sleeping gown hide her nakedness, but in no way did the soft material conceal her womanliness. Too long he dwelled upon Imogene's person, letting carnal imaginings invade, that is, until she spoke.

"I'm much better ... as you see."

He directed attention from her clothed body to the mockery showing upon her face. Not feeling anger, but a certain kinship, he replied, "Yes. I can see." Discounting prudence, he moved close, playfully saying, "And what I've seen is most pleasing."

Her puzzled look indicated she'd not caught his sexual reference, making him suspect this liberated woman was still virginal, untried. And as realization flooded her features, Seth felt, suspicions were confirmed. But, then, he couldn't really be certain.

"Please," she barely whispered, easing back to the bed and the cover's concealment. "Close the door as you leave."

CHAPTER 7

Imogene woke at day's light. She raised from cozy bedding, belonging to another. Her bare feet hit the plush carpet, and she rushed with bodily functions. The fact that she'd not left the Thomas Mansion last night caused regret—Seth's final words again verified evil designs he had on her. Hastily she washed.

"I must leave." Her whispered voice clearly sounded urgent.

Pushing aside emerald slippers and gown, she chose personal items first. After donning stockings, chemise and corset, the object of her disturbance called out and rapped upon the door.

"Miss Washington, you dressed yet?"

"Not quite," she replied. Feeling exposed, naked, at the sound of his deep voice—he dwelt just outside the room—she continued dressing.

"If you need help, I'll—"

"No, wait!" she screamed, fearful he might enter with intentions of assisting. In deceptively calmer tones, she said, "Few more minutes." Her fingers fumbled with buttons and bows.

"Then I'll not send for Ola. Grandfather requests your presence before you leave."

Remembering the kindly elder, she promptly replied, "Of course."

Hearing Seth's departing steps, relief escaped her lips. Aptly outfitted, she tidied the room and rushed downstairs.

"About time," Ola met her in the hall. "This way," the white-smocked woman said.

They walked past several rooms that were draped off from the rest of the mansion by green velvet hangings. Down marbled halls they went and through secluded sitting rooms.

"I feared you might had gone," came from inside a small, luminous area.

Adjusting vision to the room's bright yellows, Imogene recognized the elder Thomas. She smiled in salutation.

"Come, my dear," the older man said, directing her to sit close.

"I would never disregard your requests," she replied, reaching for his outstretched hands.

"Beware what you promise," he said with a teasing glint in his dark eyes which, somehow, reminded her of another.

Suddenly aware one other was present, she swirled around.

"Glad you didn't desert us, Miss Washington," Seth said, taking an opposite seat. "Grandfather, you wanted to speak with both of us." His astute gaze had only left her momentarily.

"Yes, Seth." The oldster seemed amused about something.

Her enemy's deep scrutiny made Imogene look away. Seeking diversion, she studied the room's vast, unadorned windows and gold exaggerated ceiling. Chairs and sofas, designed in French Provincial, reflected the area's white and gold colorings. Lowering eyes toward the white marbled floors, her attention quickly shifted to the two men.

"Come!" Ola had entered and stood near an adjoining eating section. "Food's ready! Don't let it get cold."

"I must leave." Imogene stood, dismissing her protesting stomach. Kinship with her enemy must be avoided. It might have adverse effect upon her avenging campaign.

"Please, my dear," the elder Thomas pleaded, reaching for her hand. "You must join us."

Considering the supplicant. how could Imogene refuse? So she followed the elder and Seth, pushing his grandfather's chair, to the readied table.

"After we eat, I'll continue our discussion," Ben Thomas said, urging her to sit at his right and Seth at his left.

As Ola rushed away, Imogene focused upon the delicious fare of ham, eggs and butter. She gave silent thanks for the older Thomas insisting upon her joining them at breakfast.

"Where's Frank?" the senior Thomas asked.

"He's not coming," Seth replied, glancing toward Imogene.

Knowing Frank didn't favor her, she suspected Seth's sorry expression had been for her benefit mostly. How could she ever forget what had happened outside the eatery? After rejecting the man's outlandish offer, he'd tagged her an ungrateful bitch.

"Are you faint, Imo—Miss Washington?" Seth said with concern.

At that inquiry, she realized her fork had slipped through trembling fingers. Shaking her head and quickly grabbing the silverware, Imogene resumed eating. Not wanting others to read distress and anger, surely, etched across her face, she kept her head downward. The egg's yolk suddenly required attention.

Ola returned with aromatic coffee and poured drinks for all; then hurried away.

"Does she ever rest?" Imogene asked, amazed at the senior woman's energy.

Seth laughed before replying, "That's normal with her."

"If Ola's not bustling about, she's ill," Benjamin agreed, pushing his plate aside. "Now we must get down to business."

She sent him questioning, anxious looks.

"Grandfather's offering you the chance to present your plead," came from Seth.

"Oh, the men I were to petition are still here?"

"They've appointed a representative."

"How? When? Who?" She turned to the speaker, Ben Thomas.

"Here and now," Seth added. "I'm selected."

Why, of all people, had her arch enemy been chosen? What did those business men fully know about her feelings toward Seth Thomas? Negative thoughts bombarded. She truly considered declining the offer and waiting for another opportunity with someone else.

"Cold feet?" the younger Thomas mocked.

"Challenges don't frighten me," she returned, accepting the dare in his eyes and words. Pushing from the table, she rose. "I'm ready ... Are you?"

Not replying, one side of his upper lip curled. He advanced, leading the way.

She followed, wondering if undertaking this feat with her foe, had been wise. Would they be alone as she petitioned? When he delivered the presentation would it be unbiased and not tainted with willingness to help? Her appeal must stand on its own merits.

"In here," Seth said, letting her go first. "This is where you would have, had you not taken ill, given the petition."

Scanning cozy surroundings, she welcomed the room's warm tones of browns, greens and tans. Padded chairs were positioned in a semi-circle around a mounted podium.

"Informal?" Seth asked, standing centered the leather chairs and smoking tables. "We can sit here."

Discretion directed she keep this formal, and distance herself—emotionally and physically—from this man. Not responding, she approached the stage and mounted two steps. Positioning behind the sturdy dais, Imogene looked out upon the auditorium as if it spectators lined the walls. Her focus settled upon front row center, where Seth waited.

"Ready?" he called.

Gathering her thoughts, she didn't answer.

"I'm waiting," he mildly taunted.

"Before I began, Mr. Thomas, I must express concern."

"Certainly," he said too condescending.

"Mr. Thomas, I want your unbiased ear, untainted with any sympathy or piety for me. You must promise to present 'our' suffrage cause honestly or I'll not make this presentation. You must swear—"

"Miss Washington," he interrupted, seemingly having taken offense. "Let me assure you, that would never happen. The funds you're requesting, after all, are not mines, but belong to absent gentlemen." His chest rose and fell before he added, "I don't mix another man's business with my personal feelings." He sat back in his chair; folded his arms and crossed his long, muscular legs, outfitted in dark knickers, hose and lace shoes. Adopted an arrogant poise, he said, "Shall we start? Or have you changed your mind?"

Brushing aside the anger he'd fanned, she breathed in and spoke confidently, relating the women's organization's origins and needs. And after some length when her lone spectator's appendages remained crossed, she feared her requests had fallen upon deaf ears. But near speech's end, his stare, which had never wavered from her, softened, and his slight frown faded. He moved forward in the chair, uncrossing his arms and legs. Had she been successful? Had she won this one against her foe?

Silence fell. He stood and studied her from head to toe.

"Well?" she said, suddenly ill at ease with his scrutiny. "What's your opinion?"

"Does it matter? You wanted it unbiased." He approached the exit. "I've heard your case. I'll present it to the men upon their return. Then you'll receive their reply." He opened the door. "My duty's done. We can go ... unless there's something you want to add."

Separating from the podium, feeling, somehow, slighted, she hurried from the stage and rushed through the opened portal. Sweeping past his waiting form and looking around for Maude's borrowed fur, she would leave.

"One moment, Miss Washington, and I'll see you home."

Imogene paused. Her slippers felt cold against the hall's marbled flooring. Like many times before, she wondered how he'd known of her unexpressed intention of leaving. Could he have this time only wanted to rid himself of her as much as she'd desired distance from him?

"Grandfather bides you Godspeed." Seth had returned with Maude's borrowed sable in his hands. Lifting the fur wrap, he held it open for her. "Presently, he's indisposed."

After slight hesitation, she stepped into the outer garment and swore heat issued from his nearness. She pulled away as if burnt and exited, not waiting for him.

Cool breezes offered relief, making her consider walking alone instead of riding with Seth. But he'd rushed past and stood at a waiting vehicle. Still icy roads beneath her silk slippers goaded acceptance. Cautiously she touched the bare hand he offered in assistance. But she quickly severed that contact when burning sensations shot through her. Luckily she managed, with some decorum, to position upon the leather seat.

After some distance, Seth stopped before the boarding house.

Imogene looked toward her new abode and wondered how her fellow traveler had known where she lived. Why wouldn't he know? This was the part of town most inhabited by women like her, unmarried, Negro and self-supporting.

"Here we are," he said.

"Yes," she replied, avoiding any help with dismounting.

"Miss Washington," he called. "I'll contact you when the men return."

Upon the porch, she paused from knocking and turned. After nodding, she rush inside, shutting out her enemy's presence.

***

For several days Seth had neither seen Imogene nor had any opportunity to confer with the men about the proposal even though they'd returned that morning. He would keep his word by having a lad notify the gentlemen about a meeting. Imogene's presentation had won him over. She absolutely had persuasive powers. But her obvious mistrust of his ability to stay objective bothered.

When mid-day came, he contacted the gentlemen in question and presented Imogene's case. Having obtained an answer, he debated if he should seek her immediately. He had promised and should, at least, make an effort to locate her. One of the boarders had told him she wasn't in residence, but on a venture at Lilly's. He directed his mount toward a dangerous part of the city when the object of his search appeared.

She, arrayed in usual long, hooded cloak, exited the house of ill-repute. Sandy-colored locks blew aimlessly until she contained them within her hood. Bounding downstairs, she began walking—he assumed to her box buggy. But, gathering her outerwear close, she continued on foot down the street. Seems her usual transportation wasn't present.

"It's late!" he called after her speeding figure. When she didn't stop, he yelled, "Miss Washington, why are you alone at this hour in this location?"

Swirling around, she stopped momentarily and replied, "What business is it of yours?" And with fluttering skirts, she continued on her way.

"You shouldn't travel this section alone and especially on foot." He'd caught up with her hastening form.

Abruptly she stopped. Pulled back her hood and pushed away wavering hair from her face. Her hazel eyes brimmed with rage as she confronted him. "Mr. Thomas, you are neither my guardian nor parent." Gasping, it appeared, for breath, she continued. "And thanks to you, I have no parent!" After pregnant silence, her voice, merging with the wind, sounded like a wail. "And Father's gone now."

Guilt resurfaced not for the part she may have felt he'd played in Bill's death, but for distress caused her. Should he wait before informing her? No, at the right time; in safer quarters, he would deliver the message. Until then, like a guardian angel, he hovered behind Imogene's fading silhouette.

Like a misty configuration, she rushed off. Her formerly straight direction took a sudden sharp turn, and he lost her. Gaining distance, his mounted figure could not take the path he believed she'd taken. Panic emerged. This part of Detroit, crawling with danger, tolerated no unattended object—human, animal or otherwise.

Not favoring leaving his horse, Seth searched the streets, waiting. And as he'd anticipated, her cloaked figure soon reappeared. He stayed in shadows, allowing her space. Before her accelerated shape became a total blur, he continued at a slow pace. When the stubborn female reached a safer area, Seth told himself, he would decide if it best to let her leave and inform her about the petition later. But obligation for the earlier promise made of informing her immediately kept him following. Once the message's delivered, he would cut all ties with the stubborn, ungrateful ... if fatherless, female.

Nearer the middle class part of town, where she resided, some relief fell over Seth. Should he catch up with the fleeting woman and give her the news? Or, considering her mood, wait? Since she didn't seem receptive, perhaps Grandfather should tell her.

Envy nagged. Seth recalled how accommodating Imogene had been toward the senior. Why couldn't she, at least, show him minimal warmth or gratitude? To hell with her! He'd done too much already for the spitfire.

Having made his decision, Seth galloped past and glanced back to nod farewell.

"Mr. Thomas, don't you have better things to do than follow me?" She had pulled back the hood, letting her hair blow wild about her angry, but appealing, features.

He stopped abruptly; dismounted and released his mount. "I was only concerned for your—"

"I have told you I don't want your sympathy or pity!"

The closer he came, the farther she moved away, making him think of some cornered lioness, seeking distance only to counterattack. Is that what drew him? Her unyielding spirit, the fire in her?

In one stride, he blocked any escape, pinning, without touching, her between himself and the entrance to a building.

Turning her face upward, she glared at him, standing her ground, saying nothing and offering, it seemed, challenge.

"You fear me," he mocked, almost believing what he had just stated. Rage in her hazel eyes caused doubt, but her full, bottom lip, quivered slightly, giving credence, he felt, to his assumption. Provocation—he attributed it to the fact that she was woman and he, man—made him glide a finger across her ample lips ever so gently.

"Oh!" escaped from her parted lips. She fell against him in obvious surprise.

He furthered contact, kissing her lips; delving his tongue in her mouth. Tasting her warmth, moistness and very essence, something, long dormant, awakened, making him grab her shoulders and pull her even closer. Reason left as he succumbed to the feel of her—Imogene, all woman, soft, warm and yielding.

Like a thirsting man, famished, Seth held her positioned between his tights. She melded perfectly with him as he reaped unrestrained havoc upon her femininity. Exposed, out in the open, they would have appeared as one shadowed form to any passerby. Luckily, streets were deserted.

With intention of carrying this to fruition—her eager and ready, flushed to him—Seth continued.

"Please,' Imogene moaned.

Ceasing activity, he slackened his hold upon her trembling form to examine her face. What he saw brought back the reality that she might have never known a man. He spied a certain vulnerability in her, almost fright. Where had the woman's usual anger and fight gone?

Confused, he released her, saying, "I'm sorry—"

"You beast!" she cried. Her combative spirit had returned, and one hand raised.

Knowing she intended smacking him, Seth halted the attack by grabbing both of her hands with his gloved ones.

"You animal. How dare you!" she screamed, striving for total detachment.

Seeing earlier fright and distress reappear in her eyes, he, gently restrained and whispered, "Imogene, forgive me. I shouldn't have—"

"You're dammed right about that!" she replied, kicking his leather boots.

If not for spurs, she might have done great damage to his shin instead of to herself.

"Oh, my God!" she cried, grabbing her foot, falling.

He stopped her descent, catching and lifting her.

"Put me down!" she demanded, squirming in his arms. "Where are you taking me?"

"Home." Flopping her upon his horse, he mounted behind. "How's your foot? he asked, reaching for the injured limb.

"No!" She slapped his hand away.

He rode off, not giving forewarning. As a result she hadn't steadied herself and slammed backwards into his body. Tightening arms around her, he let Imogene gain some control, but, not letting her break away, he directed his mount toward Second Avenue.

The boarding house came into view before he really had time relishing this woman's nearness or recalling intimacies he'd unintentionally stolen earlier. Stopping before her new residence, his hold loosened to help her dismount. But she escaped too soon and slid to the ground without his assist.

"Good night, Mr. Thomas," she sneered and hobbled up the stairs to the domicile, not looking back.

"See to that foot," he called, finding it difficult in staying angry. She seemed a sight, nearly bent over and favoring the injured limb. 'Soak it in hot water!" he called as the door slammed.

He rode off, knowing this night he would have, as usual, troubling memories of her, only this time, they would be pleasurable as well.

CHAPTER 8

Imogene ventured out days later. Her injured foot had healed enough for her to walk with less pain and a slight limp. She would see Maude soon about a concern of theirs: why hadn't she received an answer regarding her petition. The business men had returned some time ago, and Seth Thomas should have kept his promise of a prompt response. Wasn't it foolish to believe after what had happened?

Emotions stirred. She recalled how he had touched and kissed her publicly. Thank heavens, it had been dark and the streets unpopulated. Dare she be alone with him again? And why be surprised at the privileges he had taken? From the first she knew he was a scoundrel. Those feelings and sensations that still taunted must stop. Her body still warmed and trembled from his embrace. Would his individual aroma of brandy, tobacco and spice cease invading?

Shaking her head, Imogene tried dismissing memories of the man. She had no time or patience for such nonsense. More urgent matters beckoned.

Having laced the remaining Balmoral boot upon her slightly aching foot, Imogene exited the apartments. Thankful her box buggy had finally been repaired, she climbed aboard. If it had been available days ago, the incident with Seth Thomas would never have occurred. With a whack upon the horse's rump, she sped off.

"Imo—Miss Washington!" a male shouted, approaching.

Eyes fell upon the object of her condemnation, the younger Thomas. Good that they meet in the open, and not alone, in private. She waited patiently for his arrival, putting forth great effort ignoring the fine figure he made upon his stallion.

"We have unfinished business," he said leisurely; as if nothing personal had happened between them.

"I haven't forgotten!" she retorted, remembering the advances he had taken with her.

72

"The other night—" He must have recalled those offenses.

"You took unwanted privileges—"

"We must talk privately."

"Not on your life, sir." she replied, losing patience. "What you must tell me can be said here and now." Not gentling her words, she continued saying, "Anything else you can keep to yourself."

"We can't talk here." He glanced around at congregating individuals. "And I don't have the answer to your proposal. It's in a sealed envelope at the mansion."

"How convenient for you," she spat. Raising reins and clicking, she intended leaving. It seemed, the answer involving her request must wait. She would get the gentlemen's answer escorted by Maude. Her foe wouldn't dare try anything then. "I have other business now and will be at the mansion soon."

"Whenever," Seth said. Disappointment or some other like sentiment clouded his proud features as he sprinted off.

Finally continuing the short journey, Imogene spotted her friend, waiting, at the home's entrance.

"I got your message; couldn't wait!" Maude exclaimed, exchanging a brief embrace and inspecting the injured limb.

"I'm fine." Imogene followed Maude to the front parlor slightly limping and claimed her usual chair. "We must talk."

"Immie, your foot's not healed. You should still be abed." her companion reached for the injured limb.

"I'm well," she protested, easing her companion's hand away. "There's more important business needing our attention."

"The proposal." Maude smiled and waited briefly before asking, "Quickly, Immie! What's the verdict?"

"I don't know," she replied almost absently, more involved with another matter.

"Immie, what's wrong?" Maude leaned forward. "What happened?"

Not wanting to burden her fellow worker with personal problems, Imogene hesitated.

"You can tell me. I'll keep your confidence."

"I know you will," she sighed. "It's just—. He kissed me," she confessed, feeling shame's blush coloring her face.

Surprise swept over Maude's stately features. She smiled. "What man dared as much?"

"There's only one blatant enough to do that!" It angered because her friend seemed amused. "It happened in the open, outside. Well, it was dark and deserted."

After momentary silence, enlightenment struck, her ally's dark eyes, and the woman cried, "Surely, not Seth Thomas?"

"Who else?" she uttered, both irritated and embarrassed.

"All women should be so lucky," Maude literally sighed.

"How can you make light of the man's actions? He's engaged to marry soon."

"That's a farce!" Her companion had turned serious. She shook her perfectly-coifed head. "Everyone knows it. Employed by Johnetta's family, you should have witnessed Seth Thomas's polite indifference toward his betrothed. How often have the child complained about the man's rejection of her advances? She calls him her handsome eunuch."

"Eunuch!" Imogene exclaimed, disbelieving.

"Judging by your actions, you know he's anything but."

"Yes," she admitted, trying hard to ignore her companion's amusement and memories of Seth's maleness growing, pressing against her body as he'd kissed and captured her between his hard thighs. Would the man's essence ever go away?

"Are you ill?" filtered through Imogene's concentration. Maude stood, patting her shoulder. "I'll get you some tea."

"Funds are desperately needed. We must find out what decision's been made. If they've denied our proposal, other means must be employed."

"Agreed," Maude responded, abandoning former task.

"We might not get the donation." she frowned. Seth Thomas, no doubt, let prejudice against me influence his presentation."

"Then we're assured of the money." Her ally smiled.

"How can you be so certain? I told you what he did to me."

"Exactly," her confidant replied, chuckling.

Fully confused, Imogene sent her friend blank looks.

"You're such an innocent, Immie." Maude shook her head. "Have you never been with a man?"

Really baffled now, she looked away. They had never discussed such intimate matters before.

"Of course not. Or you would have known when he exposed his feelings for you that your request would have been presented favorably."

"I'm not so sure of that. He promised to stay unbiased and deliver the message honestly."

"I'm confident he tried. But, from what you have told me, the man's obviously enchanted with you and, therefore, biased."

"I don't see—" What did it matter the how or why of Seth's feelings about her? She cared less. The contents of the letter were most important. "Maude, I need you to accompany me."

"I don't understand, Immie."

Urging Maude near, Imogene explained, "The sealed envelope is at the mansion. I'll not go there alone. Our deliverance or damnation, so to speak, is in that letter."

"Am I hearing right?" Maude seemed to mock. "Hiram's prize pupil and my avowed follower permits a mere man, Seth Thomas, to deter her?"

"But—"

"If you were really in danger, I would go with you." The older woman turned serious. "How many times have I told you great sacrifices are often required for the good of any common cause?"

"You're right." Imogene knew she must withstand whatever for the goal. "Representing fellow female members, I must not appear afraid or timid. How would it look shielding myself with another?"

"Correct, Immie!" Maude embraced her. "All efforts haven't been in vain. I knew you would not disappoint."

"I'll go now." She stood; gathered her cloak and neared the exit. "I'll inform you soon as I get the answer."

"Great!" Maude hugged her again. "Seth's an honorable man. I've only heard good about him. He'll not harm you."

Imogene doubted that. Evidently she and her friend had different perceptions of harm. But she must answer the call. Making unecessary stops along the way, she ventured forth.

Pulling before the Thomas Mansion, apprehension beset. Maude should have accompanied her. But Imogene knew this must be done by herself alone. It would only make her stronger.

Eyes fell upon the stone edifice. Its massiveness, dark and overwhelming, was not unlike the home's master, Seth Thomas. Gulping several breaths while securing the box buggy, she cautiously approached the cursed place. Immediately, doors opened.

"You're expected," Frank said. "This way."

She followed to an area separated from another part of the mansion. They ventured to rooms she'd never seen before. A stone statue, naked as a newborn and poised indecently, caught her eye. She gasped and almost tripped upon her own feet from the shocking display.

Frank neither stopped nor slowed his pace. He moved fast, not looking back, and his boots barely sounded upon the floor. She must keep up or lose the way. They passed through several dark rooms that smelled of men and sin.

"Wait here!" Frank commanded, disappearing behind double, blood-red doors where men's voices echoed.

She stood in the gloomy hall waiting and regretting she'd not brought a companion.

Red portals opened, and she sighed. Even Frank's hostile presence was preferable to being isolated in these dark rooms.

"Follow me." The male voice had changed from sharp and high to soft and deep. His tall form blended with the shadows and strode ahead, not looking back.

While following the fast moving figure, Imogene sensed differences. The man now moved quieter and more like a predatory silhouette. Shock waves rippled through her body. Was this man someone other than Frank?

"I'd given you up," the shadowed figure said, keeping his back to her. "I waited." He stepped into the light, facing her.

"Seth?" she asked, taken aback at the man's new look.

His handsome features now sported a thin growth of black fuzz beneath his magnificent nose and around his sensual lips. It gave him a meaner look and lent more intensity to his eyes. But she fought threatening fear and stood her ground, holding his stare.

"Sit down, Imogene," he said, approaching and standing directly above her. "I stayed available, omitting necessities: my evening shave and change of clothing. I believed you. Hours went, and, still, I neglected urgent matters. Like a fool—"

"Visiting with Maude took longer than I anticipated," she said apologetically, wondering how and where time had gone. The man's appearance, still appealing, was ruggedly disheveled and prompted her continuing remorse. "I'm sorry."

"How is it?" he asked. Concern fell upon his features as he reached for something near her skirts.

She pulled away sharply, realizing he'd reached for the injured foot, where her hand had laid. "It's better," she said too abruptly, remembering liberties he'd taken and that they were alone. She stood. "I haven't much time. If you could give me the letter, I'll leave."

"Time?" fell from his lips. "And I've given you too much of mines."

Angry now, she replied, "Then give me the letter, and I'll take no more of your precious time."

"About the other night—" His voice and eyes softened. "I meant no harm. Have you ever been drawn to do something you wouldn't ordinarily do?"

"Of course!" she snapped. The women's movement, Maude, Professor Anderson always pushed her to broaden her horizons and do all. But how did this relate to liberties he'd taken with her?

His dark eyes turned murkier and grew more intense. He stroked her hand.

Aghast, she pulled away, severing contact. "Aren't you an engaged man, Mr. Thomas?"

"Unfortunate," he remarked. His eyes appeared clearer. "That's an obligation foolishly made."

"None the less, it's still binding!" she insisted, oddly feeling less ill at ease in this man's presence.

"Come!" he said, walking ahead. "Grandfather's waiting."

Remembering the kindly elder, she readily followed.

After they entered the hallway, he directed her differently from the direction Frank had taken her.

"I thought there only one entrance to these quarters."

"He brought you another way?" Seth asked, concerned.

"Yes." She tried sounding indifferent though still upset over his friend's coarseness.

"Respectable women are never taken that way."

"I saw why!" she declared.

Seth stopped and searched her from head to toe. He seemed to delve into her very soul.

"Something wrong?" she asked, wondering what he sought.

"I just wondered—" He shook his head, saying, "Nothing." And continued walking toward a well-lit room. "In here." He directed her ahead.

Searching, she saw the elder Thomas. He, in customary invalid chair, rested near blazing fires. She welcomed warmth and another presence.

"Welcome, my dear," Ben Thomas smiled and reached for her. "Thank you for indulging an old man by visiting with him."

"Sir, your wish is my command," she replied, placing her hands in his soft, warm ones. Comforting sensations brought back memories of happier days with the family she no longer had. Then she turned toward the man responsible, she felt, for Father's demise. But he had gone.

"Sit, my dear," the older Thomas said.

Bypassing an adjacent chair, she sat on velvet pillows and smiled up at him, much like a child would have at its grandparent's feet.

"You're the granddaughter I've always wanted," he said, still holding her hands. "Has Seth given you the letter yet?"

"Not yet." She looked hopeful. Perhaps the senior would save her the bother of dealing further with his grandson.

"By your request, my dear, the answer has remained secret and sealed. We have no idea what decision was made."

Worry cloaked her former carefree mood. But she smiled accommodatingly at the oldster. Whatever the verdict, she would deal with it. And for now she would enjoy her surroundings and the senior Thomas's company.

"Ben, it's well past your bedtime." Ola's smocked figure appeared.

Imogene frowned. The older woman neglected pleasantries and acted more like a family member than a servant. She watched the short woman push Ben Thomas from the room.

"You must excuse an old man his infirmities, my dear," Ben said, smiling. "Don't leave. Seth has your answer."

Imogene sighed, remaining seated. Her eyes examined the room. Wood-paneled walls and green-marbled fireplace lavished a certain coziness associated with friends and family. Flames danced persuasively, enhancing relaxation. Imogene's lashes, suddenly heavy, fluttered and closed.

CHAPTER 9

Another spirit touched her. She searched the shadows.

"Imogene," he whispered.

Her eyes turned toward the voice. He stood there. Fire's glow gave him an unearthly appearance. And, once again, Seth's presence stirred sensations in her.

"I should have told you sooner." His muscular form lowered to her level. Positioning upon his well-formed hunches, he gave her an envelope. "You were resting so peacefully."

She viewed his hand, long-fingered and dark, shunning its touch; recalling its feel upon her body the other night.

"Take it. Read it," he coaxed. His deep tones conjured additional memories of that same night.

With shaky hands, she eased the letter from his fingers and unsealed it. She prayed the ruling would benefit suffragettism.

"I hope it's favorable. They seemed taken with your appeal ... as was I." He touched her shoulder, dislodging the cape.

So involved with unfolding the parchment, Imogene paid scant notice to her companion's nearness. After quickly scanning the paper, she smiled appreciation. "They're granting the funds."

"I'm so glad for you." His hand stayed upon her shoulder.

"Must leave. Its late." She pulled from her foe and stood.

Retrieving the fallen cloak, he rose effortlessly and held its gray folds open for her.

"Thank you," she mumbled, still feeling obligated. Stepping into the opened garment, she lingered beneath his touch. And while his hands, like a loving vise, rested upon her shoulders, she tried to discount her actions as yielding acceptance.

"Imogene," he whispered from behind and turned her to face him. "This deserves celebration or, at least, a toast."

She stood there like a fool, captivated by his dark eyes. Her lips parted, but she neither accepted nor rejected.

"Please don't refuse, love." He'd positioned her between his hard thighs.

Hadn't she been in this situation before?

His lips descended upon hers ever so tenderly, and his tongue invaded, coaxing her teeth apart and wide. As if letting her adjust, reject his advance, he delayed the onslaught.

Why didn't she cry out or push him away? How could she stay burrowed within his body?

In delayed motion, his tongue began thrusting and teasing. His hands, roaming from her shoulders to her waist, settled just at the fullness of her hips, pulling her even closer; connecting her with his growing need; filling her with his essence and making her fall, tumbling into pleasure's abyss.

"I'm lost," she moaned, giving him free and full rein. "Hopelessly so ..."

***

Touch aroused. Hands, firm and gentle, were on her bodice, unbuttoning and loosening. Someone, a man, spoke.

"Imogene—"

Her eyes fluttered, opened and searched the haze. The room recalled another place and time. She laid upon a bed, outfitted with gold-colored coverings. One she'd laid upon before. The area's whole furnishings were familiar.

"What happened?" she asked, rising from a prone position.

"You swooned," Seth replied. He was near.

Sitting up, she became fully aware of her plight and what had previously occurred. Feeling air flow across her bosom, she looked down. One partially exposed breast peeked from her undone top and loosened stays. Panting and pulling her clothing close, she glared at him. But before she could speak, he did.

"I'm guilty," he said playfully.

"What did we—what did you do?" Imogene cried. Horrified, if he had taken favors with her—and she unconscious—he was as vile as she had labeled him and far worst.

"I only undid your dress and stays because you had fainted. You came to soon afterwards. Which proves I was correct." His voice had not rung with mockery, but brimmed with sincerity.

"I fell better," she half-conceded. "But—"

"I'm not an incubus, Imogene." He leaned closer and his perfectly formed lips widened. "I don't make love to sleeping women. When I make passionate love to you, I want you aware and participating."

The inferences and images his words caused, made Imogene blush and look away. She saw naked bodies—hers and his—moving to a silent tempo and drenched in each others sweat. This vision accelerated her from the bed to right her clothing.

"Let me help, love," he said, standing.

"No!" she shouted, nearly falling and all the while fumbling with stays and bodice.

He complied, watching her with a smile playing over his lips and a gleam in his dark eyes.

Distancing from the man's dark eyes, she turned away. Her hands lost dexterity and only succeeded in being entwined in her attire. Since she'd done this alone many times before, why couldn't she do it now? And while worrying over the quandary, fingers, dark and warm, covered hers. They gently moved hers away and took over the task.

Aptly, his hands lowered her bodice; secured stays and, purely by touch—he remained behind—his fingers fastened buttons down the front of her dress. All this had happened without words from either. But communication, hot and heavy; with touch and breath, surely occurred between both.

"Has a lover hurt you?" he whispered into her locks. He never changed his position from behind. "Is that why you're hesitant?"

"What of your wedding?" She pulled from his hands upon her waist.

"She's a promise foolishly and wrongfully made by others," he said with little emotion and no additional explanation.

"I—you shouldn't." Imogene wanted this whole affair over. She looked for her outerwear.

Seth retrieved the gray item from a chair and held it up approaching the parted garment carefully, Imogene wondered why regret lingered. When she stepped into the wool vestment and his hands rested upon her shoulders, drawing her close to his solid heat, she knew why. What woman wouldn't want his promised delights? She'd remembered Maude's declarations.

"Afraid I'll bite?" he whispered in her ear with obvious challenge.

Not one to run from confrontation, she counterattacked. "Not true!"

"Why leave then?" he taunted, keeping her near.

"It's late. Not proper. We're alone." She pulled away.

Releasing her, he asked, "Why?" In two steps, he shortened the distance between them. "What's wrong with you and me alone? Weren't you just with my grandfather?" You are a liberated woman." His voice, though mocking, felt like a caress.

"It's different with your grandfather," she protested.

"Because he's older? He's still man ... and you woman."

This man's very essence engulfed her body and soul.

"He—he—" Feeling weary, she craved escape. "I owe you nothing!" she screamed, regretting the words the instant she'd shouted them.

"Right, Imogene. You're not obligated to me." He broke contact. His demeanor turned dark and dangerous.

Feeling the ungrateful bitch Frank had called her at the eatery, Imogene knew she must apologize before leaving. Bracing herself; sweeping aside trepidations, she offered a conciliatory look and cautiously touched his forearm.

The look he gave intimidated. He said nothing.

"I'm truly sorry," she said, placing a hand upon his shirt front, as if approaching or taming a predatory, wounded beast. His heartbeat quickened beneath her fingers. She felt connection with him and knew there would be no turning back. It was too late.

***

Seth clasped the hand that laid upon his moist chest. He drew it to his lips. Gratitude welled inside, quickening his already fast heartbeat. He must capture this woman's essence, her very soul. Proceeding assuredly with kisses planted on her comely face, he uncovered other body parts and continued. Lest this elusive, creature escape, he eased her down upon the bed. Keeping near, he studied her languid form and features.

She seemed dazed and didn't speak. Her lashes fluttered, half-concealing hazel eyes.

"Are you all right?" he asked, concerned.

Her sandy-colored lashes sprung open. She appeared to have awaken from slumber, glancing from side to side till their eyes met.

"Love?"

"Yes?" Her voice sounded as if it issued from underground.

Concerned about this woman in his arms, Seth gentled and slowed his onslaught. He mustn't cause her flight. Heat and her own woman's aroma gave comfort, urging him toward their union. Hands laid on either side of her wild curls, he kissed and laved the valley between her corseted breasts. And when the elusive creature beneath him moaned, indicating, not pain, only growing need and hope of fulfillment, Seth knew they would soon connect.

For only so long could he tolerate clothed bodies. Staying attached by kissing, he undid her bodice and corset. Her hands wedged between his, helping with disrobing. Momentarily stunned, he'd feared she might, just at consummation, resist and run. If she told him to stop, no matter how difficult, he would. He wanted no woman he must force.

After discarding his shirt, he neglected other attire for now. Imogene must be fully submissive first and begging. And once they were joined, their bodies, hot, bare, near exploding, would doubt cease.

"Seth," she barely said. "I'm afraid. Strange sensations overwhelm—"

Severing their connection long enough to remove remaining clothing, he whispered reassuringly, "Soon, my love."

"Where are you?" she called.

"I'm here," he replied, answering her call and clasping her searching hands. As he attempted to divest her of one remaining item, her chemise, faltering akin to fright seemed to beset her.

"I don't know. What—what will happen?" she moaned.

"Trust me, love," he pleaded, kissing and caressing her swollen lips and ripe breasts. Nothing must impede, not with the goal so near. "I'll show you the way, my love," he sighed, readying her for their coupling.

"Maybe we shouldn't—"

He entered her with one thrust, cutting off her cry with his mouth. And when tears pooled in her hazel eyes and spilled down her face, he knew she had been—as suspected—a virgin, untouched by any man until him. Too late to stop. No time for apologies, he forged ahead, slowing only long enough for her to adjust. With the one goal in sight, reaching the summit together, Seth exercised great restraint. He moved inside her copious heat and urged her on with sweet utterances that sounded like whispered moans.

As her need grew and her hips rose, matching his moves, Seth felt moist heat turning to gripping fire. Control seeped away. Both cried out each other's name, having climaxed and reached the apex together.

Lingering over and inside her, he said, "You should have told me."

"Told you what?" Her eyes flashed open, displaying murkiness.

"That you'd never been with a man."

"What difference would it have made?" she retorted. Her old spirit had returned.

"The difference in how much pain I caused you," he replied, amused at her spunk and innocence.

"Oh," was all she mumbled, looking and turning away.

"Sleep, my love," he sighed into her unruly curls, pulling her even closer even though she kept her back to him. All would be well between them now ...

***

"Where is she?" he bellowed, entering the hallway while securing the gold-colored robe over his nakedness.

"She left near day, Seth."

He turned to see Frank with that irritating smirk plastered across his pale, lean features.

"Taking my advice doesn't seem to have helped your mood. It's nastier than ever. Didn't she satisfy?"

In two strides he was upon his faithful pal and slammed a fist into the man's narrow jaw. As Frank fell, dislodging his Stetson, Seth felt regret—recalling when Bill had fired perilously close to his partner's head. He offered the downed man assist, apologizing with, "Sorry, friend. Don't know what came over me."

Frank accepted his extended hand. He stood, retrieving his hat. "A she-devil like Imogene Washington will drive any man crazy."

Not any man, just me, Seth thought. He returned to the place where he had made love to Imogene. There, perhaps, he'd find some solace, breathing in her lingering scent and reliving the passion he and that damn, slippery, she-viper had shared!

CHAPTER 10

Imogene stayed abed well pass noon after leaving the man who had done things to her—she blushed recalling. She'd moved away, reluctant at leaving, but knowing she must. Being with Seth had felt too right. His body, strong and warm, had enclosed hers, making her feel needed, cherished, alive. Now she knew what Maude had meant by "delights".

Because of the late hour and fear he might venture there, she'd not returned to her residence, but had gone to Maude's. Her friend had accompanied her to guest rooms and had had good sense to leave after asking about her well-being.

Wanting to keep Seth's essence near, she had disrobed fully and climbed between the covers, not washing. Tears had fallen, not for lost virginity—that neither mattered nor dictated her worth. Weeping had been for turmoil and havoc Seth Thomas had created in her very soul; her whole being—it still loitered within her bosom. He had succeeded where no other man had and shaken her orderly world and made her reconsider not forsaking all for the suffrage cause.

Imogene had forgotten his pending marriage. But, now, she remembered, and it hurt, causing guilt and regret. Would or could he abandon an obligation—however unfortunate or not wanted—made by others? If he did not wed Johnetta, the girl's father, Mr. Johnson, a wealthy man, assuredly, would destroy him and all he held dear. There was only one choice for her: to be his mistress.

"Never, never!" she declared, pulling covers over her head, muffling her cries.

Remorse lessen, somewhat, and when sleep came, she knew suffrage causes must remain paramount and Seth Thomas avoided at all costs. For when he married and family occupied his life, she prayed, life must improve for all, especially herself.

Breathing in his individual odor, lingering upon her body, in her pores, thoughts turned inward, and she dreamed about her and Seth making love.

When she awaken, near dusk, Imogene washed and dressed in fresh apparel provided by Maude. She shared the evening meal with the Graves and was thankful conversation stayed impersonal. She had planned upon returning to her rooms at the boarding house after the meal, but considered attending an informal affair with mutual friends. Needing diversion, especially now, she agreed to accompany Maude. So having been rushed from the house by Mr. and Mrs. Graves, she and Maude ventured forth.

"Here we are," Imogene announced as they pulled before a Victorian style, powder-blue and pink abode. After what had happened between her and Seth, men were the last people she wanted to encounter or see, she asked, "Just women will attend?"

Before her companion answered, a knowing, but sympathetic look passed over her friend's features. "Only the usual feminine group, Immie."

Smiling in response, she followed her ally to the entrance.

"Come in!" Phyllis Bently directed when the door opened. "I have a surprise for you two!"

Having shared many small gatherings with the tiny, joyous female, Phyllis, Imogene felt this affair would be no different. They would probably discuss feminine matters, drink tea and indulge in the woman's luscious pound cake. Depositing outerwear with their host, they gathered in the cozy parlor and exchanged greetings with three other fellow members named Minnie, Esther and Blanche who ranged in hues of coffee, cocoa and creme.

Imogene claimed her favorite position upon a cushioned sofa. She sunk into the flowered seat, welcoming the sense of comfort spreading over her. She smiled as Maude sat near. How good it felt to be with female workers and no men were present to interfere or flaunt their egos.

"Ladies," Phyllis announced. "I have a surprise. There's a well-known female citizen asking to join our ranks."

Imogene's head searched the room with others. She detected no new faces.

"She'll arrive soon," Phyllis began pouring tea from an ornate silver pot. "The woman has influence and money. And that can only greatly enhance the cause."

"What's her name?" Imogene asked, unable to await the woman's arrival.

"Honey," a male voice interrupted, drawing all attention to Phyllis's handsome spouse. He presented his wife's savory cake. "Greetings and excuse me, ladies," he said, placing the confection upon a table in their midst.

"Thank you, James dear," Phyllis purred, blowing her spouse a kiss as he left.

This scene had occurred in Imogene's presence often. Then why did she feel envy and regret now? She never had before.

"Cursed man!" she emitted, recalling recent happenings with Seth.

"You all right, Imogene?" Maude asked, concern showed upon the woman's face.

Shaken from reveries, Imogene realized her words had been heard. She felt the flush of embarrassment upon her face and whispered, "Nothing, I'm fine."

Conversation quickly turned to other matters as Phyllis distributed pieces of her pound cake. China, silverware and chatter resounded as all ate and exchanged small talk. Even Imogene's former worries dissipated. She relaxed and laughed readily at every humorous comment.

"Honey." James appeared at the entrance. "Another guest is here."

Their hostess departed and quickly returned with a slender woman, dressed in elegant ware. "Ladies, I present our new member. You all know her."

Imogene gasped, viewing the woman from behind. Her tiny. perfect form was too recognizable.

"Hello, Imogene and Maude," the new recruit said, turning around.

Thankful Maude welcomed the young girl first, granting Imogene additional time, she inhaled and faced the future bride of the man who, recently, had made love to her. Feeling like Judas, she managed a smile and welcomed Johnetta into their organization. And when their new co-worker chose a nearby seat, Imogene knew she must leave.

"What's wrong?" some asked when she stood.

"I can't stay," she replied, moving toward the exit. "There is an urgent matter I must attend."

"I'll accompany you," Maude said, following. "We'll see our way out, Phyllis."

Properly outfitted, she and Maude left, boarding the box buggy. While on route neither conversed. And when they arrived at her companion's home, Maude did not dismount.

Seeing her friend's troubled expression, Imogene offered no explanations.

"Do you need to talk, Immie?"

"Not now." She turned from her friend's caring eyes.

"When you're ready, I'm here." Maude dismounted.

"Of course," she said to the departing figure, grateful her colleague had not pursued the matter.

The journey continued with thoughts of how to regain order in her life and, somehow, eradicate Seth Thomas from it. As conjured by memories of him, the man's mansion came into view. Her gaze strayed to the overpowering, stone structure. A lone light shown from one window. The part, she knew, where his club members gathered.

Sighting sudden movement near the entrance, alarms sounded in her head. She gave heed and speeded up, recalling what had occurred there so recently. Yes, she gained distance from his residence, but not from memories of him or what they'd done privately.

He stayed with her like strong aroma that would neither ware off nor wash out. Once touched by him, would she ever return to before? Or would he haunt her forever?

Imogene sought privacy once horse and buggy were housed for the night. She must give a speech at United Methodist, and reviewing the presentation made more sense than pondering over a man she had no right to. And if she had any attraction for him—which she definitely didn't want—the man was promised to another. Seth Thomas, above all, must be avoided and uprooted from her life.

"Imogene, you have company," one of the female roomers called from the hall.

Believing Maude had come to assist with tomorrow's speech, she hurried to the receiving parlor.

"You left?"

Freezing just at the room's entrance, Imogene prayed the speaker, her guest, was not the very person she'd recently vowed to avoid and uproot from her life.

Seth's magnificent form approached. He was garbed in dark coat and trousers and demanded, "Why did you leave?"

"Does it matter?" she replied, believing the man referred to the time after they'd made love. "You got what you wanted!"

"I meant tonight. But since you brought it up—" He drew her inside the parlor and, with a booted foot, shut the door. Keeping her near, he added, "You were totally against and innocent of what happened between us?

"I never—of course—but!" Thoughts converged. She could not express them. Yes, she had not pursued him, and she had for the first time experienced something grand and unique with him. But he was promised to another.

"You found our joining repulsive," he mocked more than asked, pulling her even closer.

Too near; captured in his arms, she said nothing. His broad chest, not quite flattening her full breasts, induced feelings and recallings best kept dormant. She let this man do things again to her she swore would never happen again. Her whole being savored all he gave. His lips and hands hushed every protest, making her submissive and ready. Prior promises, all forgot, had been empty and hollow.

"Lock up time!" the landlady called from behind closed doors. The woman's quick steps approached and dissipated.

"Oh!" Imogene pulled from the her night caller. "You must leave."

"One last kiss before I go," he said playfully, reclaiming his former hold.

"Goodnight, Seth." She warded him off, escaping into the hall.

"Until tomorrow," he called after her departing figure.

"Not on your life," she whispered only after reaching private rooms and once securely behind closed doors. But physical distance did little in keeping him emotionally or mentally from her.

For too long she stayed glued to the closed door listening for his good-bye and departure. Hearing the outer door's closing, her feet made haste toward the opened window. Behind partially separated drapes, she spied him mounting his black stallion. His figure, a tall shadow, rode off, and something inside, felt torn apart. Shuddering, from the sensation, she gripped her middle and vomited. She whispered, "What if—?"

Why had she permitted him so close? Because he held powers over her? How dare she even consider such an excuse! He had neither forced nor drugged her. Weary over mounting obstacles, Imogene sought diversion. Her eyes fell upon papers scattered across the bed.

Not inclined, but knowing her speech was tomorrow, she gathered parchments and started mulling through them. Ideas would not focus. They only wavered back and forth from her speech to Seth Thomas. Out of frustration, she let the document slip from her fingers and sail to the carpet. She sighed, sinking to the bed. But Seth's allure persisted even as she pulled covers close and closed her eyes, blocking out visible objects.

Would rest forever elude? Solace must come. But in the dark which should have brought repose, the object of distress, materialized. And like a vision, his perfect outline, tall and ebony, solidified. So once again, she succumbed and reveled in memories of their lovemaking.

Would her torment be this forever? Seth Thomas, promised to another, could only give unwedded bliss. And she, advocating women's rights, could accept nothing less than marriage. Imogene vowed, anew, she would concentrate upon suffragettism and avoid the man at all costs. But a voice inside taunted, Liar! The minute you see him, your're lost.

CHAPTER 11

He departed the boarding house elated. Once again, Imogene had come into his life, and she'd, if reluctantly, let him hold and kiss her. But he had arrived at the mansion in a dejected mood. An insurmountable problem confronted him now. After this encounter with the elusive creature, Seth knew he could not remain passive or sacrifice himself to the promise his parents had made with the Johnsons years ago.

Dismounting, he approached his residence. Once inside, he tossed aside his bowler, greatcoat and leather gloves. His plight called for trustworthy advise.

"Back already?"

Seth's attention shifted from pressing concerns to Frank. His and the man's relationship had suffered since Imogene slipped away after they'd first loved. Several times Frank had insisted he'd forgotten their confrontation. But Seth knew his partner still held that against him. Wanting to make amends, he viewed Frank hopefully. Would his buddy give needed counsel?

"How did it go?" Frank leaned his slim frame against the door jam. A glass of amber liquid rested between his long, claw-like fingers.

"Let's talk," Seth said, going toward an isolated place. Once behind closed doors, he perched upon the desk and loosened his neck scarf. "There are matters weighing on my mind."

"I'm not surprised," Frank said, taking a sip of his drink. "Maybe you should have steered clear of her."

"Too late for that now," he admitted.

Alarm mushroomed across Frank's face. "What did she do? No woman's ever had such power over you!"

Seth's naturally deep tones felt like gut wrenching sighs. "What am I to do? I can't marry Johnetta."

"Why not? Keep Imogene for your mistress." Frank swallowed all his drink.

"I want her as my wife, no more, no less."

"Are you serious? Frank banged his glass upon the desk, causing it to skid across the desk, stopping just at the edge.

"I'm damn serious."

"Do you know what you're saying? We're condemned! Don't you know what Johnetta's father will do?"

"I can't forget. But I must have Imogene."

"Didn't you accomplish that the other night?" his partner jeered playfully.

If Seth'd not found his plight crucial, he might have better tolerated Frank's flawed humor. But there was nothing funny about this predicament.

"The other night gave and revealed more than expected," Seth confessed, remembering shared passion and added proofs of Imogene's virginity smeared upon his sheets. "Still ... that was only for an evening. I want her for a lifetime. She be my wife, and God willing, have my children."

"You're crazy! Frank's bulging eyes made those words more applicable to him. "Old man Johnson'll never release you from that promise or let you hurt his only child. After you wed Johnetta, Imogene can still be your life-long companion, mistress—whatever you call her. And both women can have your children. You really want to support that many households?"

"You've offered me no option or any I want," Seth replied, shaking his head.

"You want Johnetta completely out of the picture and that ungrateful B—"

"Don't say it!" Seth shouted, ready to slam his partner.

"You do have a problem, friend," Frank replied stony-faced while backing up.

Seth found his own mood, not improving, but darkening.

"If you don't marry Johnetta, her father'll destroy us—you. What of your grandfather and Ola?"

"Therein lies the problem. They're innocent." Approaching the sideboard, he reached for the decanter of brandy and poured himself a drink. After swallowing the contents, he turned to his companion. "You and I could make it on our own."

"What are you gonna do?"

"Don't know." He turned to leave. His partner had been little help. Solace might open better solutions.

"Is she worth it, Seth?"

He turned toward his partner, studying the man's drawn features. He saw no reason to reply. The man knew his feelings.

"Is Imogene Washington worth our destruction?"

How could he answer? To lose or harm her was equal to his own demise. If others weren't involved, Ola and Grandfather, no problem would exist. But things were never simple. He exited.

"The woman's ruining you, Seth."

He continued walking, ignoring Frank's caution.

"Beware the hard-hearted, she-devil," his comrade shouted "She's winning!'

Seth felt, after his and Imogene's one and only physical union, she was much less a threat. Hadn't she given fully, allowing and sharing love with him? She had matched his every move and cried out his name as he'd uttered hers. Future couplings—there would be many more—promised even a stronger bond between them. Yes, even if she denied or fought those feelings, he knew he'd sealed his mark upon her.

Recalling how the woman had sneaked off and ran away after that intimacy, he smiled at her stubbornness. She might deny and fight it now, but one day she would admit they were made for one another, and do all to advance that togetherness.

Those thoughts brought back pressing problems of a vow made. His father had obligated him when he, not of age, and Johnetta, a mere babe, weren't concerned about adult things. He didn't know full details of the agreement made between his parent and Mr. Johnson, the caretaker. Grandfather had only said it involved money and property. And if he broke the oath, dire consequences would befall the entire Thomas family.

Therein existed his dilemma. A promise made by another binding him to wed Johnetta, a mere child he barely tolerated.

He'd accepted the obligation indifferently. At that time he'd cared little for the few women used to mostly slack a young man's sexual curiosity. But now a stubborn, beguiling female had come into his life and disrupted that complacent acceptance.

How could he not wed Johnetta or live without Imogene?

Since answers eluded him, Seth abandoned aloneness and sought companionship. Frank's morbid ridicule he did not want. At this hour, Ben and Ola slept. And the one person, Imogene, he craved solitude with, he'd been forced to leave. Would she see him this late? No doubt she slept. Picturing the female wrapped in covers, his spirits lightened, and he began humming some love tune. Did her thoughts dwell upon him as his lingered over her?

***

Moaning echoed, breaking through the dark. A bundled form tossed and turned like a lone vessel in a storm pitched sea. Momentary quiet came. But the covered shape still rotated about the bed in silence.

Imogene had awakened long ago, remaining semi-conscious, fighting reflections of Seth. unsuccessfully she had lamented and shifted upon the bed. The man's image, his very essence, would not leave her. No matter how much she affirmed she cared nothing for him, his powerful image consumed her. Like black enveloping white, his image remained. Why keep making it hard on herself? They could never be together, not in this life. She knew that.

She rose, seeking light and some task to busy her hands. Once she lit the kerosene lamp and claimed unfinished sewing upon the bedside table, Imogene rested against the headboard. Her fingers sorted out pink ribbon and delicate lace for application to silk underthings for Johnetta, no doubt for the young woman's approaching marriage.

"Ouch!" she cried, accidentally pricking her finger with a needle. Thoughts of Seth removing those garments at his and Johnetta's nuptial night had caused the carelessness. Unable to cope, she flung the chore aside and put the injured finger between her lips. Mostly out of frustration, she sucked the digit longer and harder than necessary. Because the sensations felt and the noises heard reminded her of when she and Seth had made love, Imogene found a clean rag and secured it around the slight cut.

Knowing she must be strong and not let Seth Thomas—or any man—have such an effect upon her, Imogene sought papers she and Maude had prepared for a speech to be given in the afternoon. As she sorted through scribbled notes, attention turned from the owner of the Thomas Mansion and concentrated upon suffrage, every woman's right.

After reviewing her discourse at length, she felt a little less troubled. Seth and his entrapments must be avoided at all costs. Involvement with and total commitment to the movement offered the best solution for her troubles. Had she any other choice?

Being his mistress was out of the question.

The full light of day broke through as she opened drapes to peer outside. With spring coming and the wedding fast approaching, her troubles would be over. Once Seth married, she hoped, prayed, the man, needing to be more discreet, would find it harder to approach or devise ways to engage her in intimacies. Yes, given time, life would return as it was before Seth Thomas.

***

Days turned into weeks. Winter had gone and became spring. And in that time, Imogene had, somehow, eluded the tall, dark man, Seth Thomas. There had, of course, been near meetings, but she had escaped his perceptive eyes and thanked her good fortune. So why still question what duty or person— perhaps female—had kept him away? Scolding herself for such foolishness—sexual intimacy between her and him could not continue—she hurried from her rooms. Day's duties called.

***

"What's troubling you?"

Seth looked up from papers scattered across his desk. Not responding immediately, he studied his ally's angular, still attractive features. Not seeing the man's usual mockery, he didn't answer.

"Closer the wedding, the darker your mood turns," Frank said. "You stay locked in your rooms."

"I haven't seen her lately." Seth pushed aside pen and stationary.

"Why do I know you're not talking about Johnetta?" Frank perched upon the desk's corner.

"It's that obvious?" Seth replied, wondering if his pal's words, devoid of usual bite, were really sincere.

"You barely put up with Bill, her father, but, more like that man than not, you can't get enough of his daughter."

"True," he admitted. "Love's blind."

"A good roll in the hay with someone else might—"

"No," Seth interrupted. "I want no other woman but Imogene."

A troubled look covered Frank's face.

"What am I to do?" Seth stood, wanting resolution to this problem. Bypassing the container of brandy, too clearly in abundance, he approached green draperies, parted them and glanced outside. "Spring's here. The wedding's near," he said while viewing radiant sun, greening trees and budding flowers.

"She's doing you a favor, staying away."

"How? Since her absence, she's a wound in my heart."

"Marry Johnetta and keep Imogene as your mistress."

"Second best won't do for her nor me."

Frank shrugged, saying, "My friend, you are in a pickle."

"Hell!" Seth murmured, hurling the drapes shut. The velvety material continued swaying, it seemed, from his voice's deepness and his passion. "Tell me something I don't know!"

"She's speaking at the church this afternoon." Frank offered as he left.

Seth knew his partner's information referred to Imogene and the neighborhood church, the only Methodist congregation attended by their race and where his marriage would take place soon. He had an appointment with the pastor. What if he happened upon the evasive maiden while there?

Making haste, Seth changed into fresh clothing. For too long, she had slipped from sight, at least, from his. Others had told him of her whereabouts after the fact. Expected joy surfaced in his smile. Just to see her again since their first and only coupling, rushed his departure.

But hurting anger flared. He remembered how she'd slithered away while he'd slept. No matter. He would see her again. And perhaps they would share love again.

Freshly attired, Seth dismounted and entered the church. Hearing women voices down the corridor, he ventured in that direction. Several females of various shapes, hues and ages were conversing and seeking seats. Quiet fell as one stately female, approached the podium. When that person turned, facing him and the audience, Seth smiled in satisfaction. The object of his search, Imogene, stood there. Checking his pocket watch, he saw he had some leisure to behold his lover.

Determination danced over her alluring features. Her hazel eyes, stared, unblinking, and her lips, lavishly formed, parted. Seth felt tightening in his groin as he took in all of her dark-clothed form—flesh he had bared, touched, worshipped. Her speech about female matters he gave little heed. Interest stayed upon her; what they had shared; if they would join again physically. Her wayward locks awakened memories of how she had appeared after lovemaking with her sandy-hued hair laying upon the sheets.

Reluctantly Seth pulled away. If he stayed longer, he would miss the appointment.

"Wondered if I might find you here," the minister said.

"Sorry, Reverend. I—"

"Right down the hall," the man of God said, leading the way to his office. "I know you're anxious to have this marriage business over."

Feeling bitter remorse at those words, Seth cursed his deceased parent, once again, for promising him to Johnetta so long ago. Why should he feel guilty over wanting or be denied the only woman he must have? But for Grandfather and Ola, he would forsake business and wealth to wed Imogene. But things were different. He must honor the commitment. Following Rev. Morris to the office, he closed the door, shutting out Imogene's voice, and discarded his bowler upon a vacant chair.

Hours passed. Seth kept forcing attention back to the business at hand: his and Johnetta's nuptials.

"Well, my instructions are over," Pastor Morris said, extending a brownish hand. Smiling, the stocky man asked, "Have you other problems?"

Seth had already stood, ready for communion with Imogene. But he studied the preacher's kindly face and almost confessed his feelings for a woman other than his intended. Discretion kept him silent. Losing true love—what he had for Imogene- -was no sin and would be a greater tragedy if lost.

"No, Pastor." Clasping the man's firm grip, Seth thanked the fatherly man and left.

Quiet came from the room where the women had gathered earlier. He swore, "Damn, she's eluded me again!

He must see her, and the hour was not late. Increasing his stride, he sprinted down the hall, ignoring feelings he'd forgotten something. Once outside when breezes hit his bare head, Seth remembered his forgotten bowler. Cussing quietly, he retraced his steps. Rushing down the dim hall, he bumped an emerging figure. "Excuse—"

"Oh!" The person exclaimed, turning toward him.

"Imogene!" he cried, grasping her forearms to keep both of them from falling.

"I thought you'd gone." Frustration clouded her features.

Not releasing, but pulling her closer, he taunted, meaning every word, "You can run from our love for only so long."

CHAPTER 12

"Ple—please—Seth," she whispered halfheartedly.

"Do you know how long I've craved, waited for, this moment, my love?" he uttered between kisses.

"Someone might see us." She pushed, really caressed, placing her palms upon his hard chest. She felt his heaving bosom, in perfect rhythm with hers. His heat ignited, burning her insides. If he continued his plundering, Imogene would surrender right there, in this holy place.

"You have forgotten more than you hat."

Seth abandoned the hold upon his prize reluctantly.

"Rev. Morris!" they both cried.

She saw no blame in the pastor's eyes. Only tolerance was mirrored there. Clutching shawl and books closer, she sought escape.

'Thank you," Seth said, capturing his bowler while keeping an eye upon her. "I must take full blame for this."

"Are you certain you have no other concerns?" the minister asked. His hands were positioned as if in prayer across his rounded middle.

"There are matters that need attention," Seth admitted. "But who has the answers?"

Seeing opportunity for escape, she turned away and approached the exit.

"Let us talk," the minister said, looking at her; including her in his invitation.

"But—" she protested, moving away.

"This has nothing to do with her," Seth interrupted.

In all honesty, Imogene could not agree, but rushed off nonetheless, thankful Seth had intervened.

Clement weather embraced her as she boarded the box buggy and ventured homeward. She had escaped once again. If they had continued, she knew her body would have betrayed, and she would have given into resulting desires—his and hers. Not blameless or denying attraction for Seth, she only knew, at all costs, the man must be avoided.

How had feelings for him switched from loathing to the opposite extreme of—she feared thinking the word—love?

As if someone or something pursued her, Imogene urged her horse faster. In her haste, she nearly collided with approaching vehicles and, as a result, she continually offered apologies to several irate drivers.

Pulling before the boarding house, she hurried inside and welcomed the solace her rooms would give. Once between private walls and behind locked door, she threw aside her shawl. As the flowered material landed upon the bed, she discarded her books there also. Several moments of rest should refresh she believed as the publications sunk into the thick bed covering.

"Imogene, you have a visitor," sounded with a rap outside closed doors.

"Rest must wait," she whispered, turning from the bed's invite. "Yes," she called, opening the door.

"In the front parlor," one of the female tenants, Betty, said, turning away. The woman's stripped skirts rustled and switched as she hurried away.

Shutting her doors, Imogene paced down the hall. Her booted feet tapped across polished floor boards. She could only imagine her visitor to be Maude. And needing confidential talk, namely involvement with Seth, her steps quickened toward the waiting visitor.

"Feared you might not come and would have sent excuses."

She jumped and backed away, recognizing his deep voice. But he gently coaxed her into the room, closing the glass doors, preventing any escape.

"Come, love," he urged, bringing her down beside him upon the cushioned sofa. "We must talk."

Allowing him to keep hold of her hands, she nervously awaited his words.

"What can we do?" he barely whispered, searching her face. "We have troubles."

"The problem's yours, not mines," she uttered, looking away and praying he'd not read the lie in her eyes. Because, no matter what she said, her feelings for him had changed. She did care.

"My wooing's not been in vain." He lifted her hands and searched her very soul. With elevated conviction, he said, "You do care for me."

"No!" she cried, reclaiming her hands. How had he known? How could she keep from lying and deny feelings for him? She, an accomplished speaker, found no words. Her hands entwined till they ached.

"Imogene—" Seth gently undid her fingers, digit by digit. "Love is not a crime."

"But it is for us," she said more from regret than belief.

"Why?"

"Your pending marriage—"

"Regrettable." His voice reeked with sorrow and anger.

She no longer resisted his pull. Nor did she stop him from kissing her sweating palms. The dark texture of his lips felt like velvet against her flesh. Chills surged through each fiber of her being. Fire ignited within and made her consider succumbing.

"Why do you hinder my every advance," Seth pleaded.

"We have no right." She dodged the pain in his dark eyes. "Our actions will harm blameless others."

Her last statement must have worked. Hurt disappeared from his handsome features. Concern took its place. He no longer pursued her.

Silence prevailed as they sat upon the sofa, not touching.

"If not for Grandfather and Ola, I would risk all to make you fully mines, my love."

Imogene thought it good he should include the maid, Ola, with regard for his grandfather. And had his last statement, making her fully his, meant marriage? Of course not! She had neither money nor position. Satisfying carnal desire had been his sole motivation. Believing this made her next words easy.

"It's late, Mr. Thomas." She stood. "You must leave.

"Don't turn formal on me!" he demanded. "You care."

He spoke truth, but she wouldn't be any man's mistress. If he knew so much—even her deepest thoughts—he knew this.

"There's no need for further discussion. We can never be. Stolen moments will only prolong agonies which must end in separation." Approaching French doors, she turned the crystal handle. She must distance from him.

"Love," he pleaded, covering her hand with his.

"Please—" she implored, shunning, in vain, the man's nearness. His warmth and strength enveloped, making her feel one with him. If she didn't separated immediately from this man, there would be no turning back. Her hands pushed against his hard, broad chest, she pleaded, "Please, Seth."

"Tell me you don't care and there's no love in your heart for me," he taunted, keeping her near. "Say it!"

She tried, but the lie wouldn't come. Out of frustration her head fell against his solid chest. And once again, she felt security she'd not felt since before Mother's death. With great effort, she stifled sobs, welling up in her throat and gushing from her soul.

"You can't say the lie," he mocked, elated. After some minutes, he held her at distance. "I'll leave now and give you privacy." Snatching his bowler from a side table, he exited. "I know your answer, Imogene and will act accordingly."

Reeling from their too current encounter, she watched his magnificent figure disappear. Exhausted, not analyzing his last statement, she ran to her rooms.

"Dinner's waiting for you, Imogene," the landlady called.

"Not hungry," she mumbled, escaping behind closing doors.

***

Seth had hoped for more in his encounter with Imogene. He hadn't shared what he'd hoped, but he'd discovered something suspected all along. After tossing his bowler hat aside, he sought companionship.

"No frown. Must have gotten what you wanted," Frank stated.

"Not really," Seth revealed.

"Could have fooled me."

"I found out one thing." Not getting her into his bed a second time, he wouldn't mention. "Imogene's much less a threat"

"That's good if it's true," Frank sneered. "Since you've bedded her, should be easy getting her to be your mistress."

"Therein is my trouble. I want her for wife."

"Does it matter what woman you prefer? Marry maidenly Johnetta and quiet your lusts with Bill's stubborn daughter."

"Have you cared for another more than your own self?"

His companion shot him a look that seemed, for only a second, to indicate he had or did, but it was quickly replaced with the man's usual grin. "Not gone crazy yet."

Realizing he would get no practical advice from Frank, he said, "I'll be with Grandfather if you need me."

"Doubt I will. No one's arrived yet," It was just as well they had no members. He needed an understanding ear because Rev. Morris had instructed him, for the greater good, to forsake the very woman he couldn't live without. Seth worried over some solution to his dilemma. Wedding day, fast approaching, only increased the need for resolution.

Entering the library, scents of old books, lemon-polish and warmth from smoldering embers in the gigantic fireplace enticed.

"Frank put Ben to bed earlier. He didn't feel well," Ola said, not looking up from mending.

"Anything serious?" he asked.

"You never know with Ben. His constitution's funny. I gave him my special tea."

He stood, with hands in his knicker pockets, wondering if Ola might be receptive. His aunt often referred to love as tomfoolery and seldom discussed such things with him.

"Won't grow any taller, nephew." She directed him to sit.

Doing as ordered, he heistated, not saying what he wanted.

"Well." She put aside her mending. "What's bothering you?"

He sent puzzled looks her way.

"You remember when I found you wacking the heck out of my flowers?"

Recalling the incident, he nodded. Upset over a favorite, misplaced toy, he'd vented frustration upon his aunt's roses. Scolding him for destroying a thing of beauty, the woman had gathered him into her ample lap and wiped away his tears and given relief. Might she help him now as well?

"It's about the marriage agreement."

"Thought as much," she said in her complacent way and looking him in the eye.

"There's someone else"

"That girl that took sick," Ola interjected.

"Imogene—" Seth supplied.

"The old man who died here, his daughter."

Amazed at Ola's accurate perception, he nodded.

"They should have told you everything long ago." She began the story. "Your father was in danger of losing everything. Had to do with investments. Don't know much about those things. But to save the family from the poor house, your father got a lot of money in exchange for the promise of you and Johnetta marrying."

Seth had heard this from questionable sources. Now Ola had verified the fact. But this information helped little. Innocent others would suffer no less. He must take Johnetta as spouse and forsake the woman he wanted.

"Well," Ola said, interrupting concentration. "It's bedtime." She gave him a hasty kiss upon the forehead and hurried away.

For hours and even when he heard male voices—denoting members had arrived—Seth remained secluded in the library. His head pounded, making him rest it against the soft leather chair's high back.

"Seth." Frank's voice jarred. "It's day."

"Day?" He said, looking toward dawn's light peeking through the library windows. "How long have I slept?"

"Judging by the looks of you, not long enough." Frank took an adjoining seat.

"Nothing's been solved to my satisfaction."

"So it seems."

'If only blameless others weren't involved."

"There's only one choice. You must marry Johnetta."

Uttering yes gave sickening finality to his tribulations, and Seth only lowered his head in mock resignation.

"Things could be worst, friend," Frank whispered, giving an encouraging pat upon his sagging, aching shoulders. "It'll be over soon."

Barely hearing his partner's soft stride and the door's closing, He must freshen up and shave. Duties called regardless of his feelings or desires. I must keep up a brave front, he told himself. But how, without Imogene?

CHAPTER 13

"I'm worried about you, Immie."

Maude's voice shattered concentration, but was most welcome. The past weeks had wrecked destruction upon Imogene. Dodging someone who occupied her dreams and invaded every thought required constant battle, and she, near wit's end, required illumination or some hope.

"Happy you came," she replied, pushing aside papers and making room for her friend to sit upon rumpled covers. "Come join me, Maude."

"Immie, no one's seen you for awhile." Worry clouded Maude's proud features as she took the indicated seat.

"I've been so busy." Imogene fingered scattered parchments she had pushed aside.

'I weren't aware you had an upcoming speech," Imogene's mentor said.

"I have none. I—I just—." No longer able to keep a lying front, she fell against her companion's lace-covered bosom and sobbed, "Oh, Maude, what am I to do?"

"I felt something was wrong, but I never guessed you were this distraught."

"It'll end in another week," she said, suddenly feeling like a silly child. How useless to wallow in sorrow because of circumstances beyond her control? She moved from her friend.

"Does this have to do with Seth and Johnetta?"

Not responding, she looked away.

"I've said before, that whole affair's nonsensical and should have never been. There must be something you can do."

"What?"

"There's still time!" Maude jumped up in a flurry of silk skirts. Searching through closets and compartments, she presented fresh underthings and a creme-colored dress. "Put these on!" she commanded. "You're paying Seth Thomas a visit."

"I can't," she insisted, pushing aside the clothing.

"Why?"

"Seth has no choice. He must marry Johnetta."

"Foolishness!" Maude insisted, urging her to dress after retrieving the discarded clothing and nearly tore Imogene's attire from her body, thrusting fresh articles at her. "Dress!"

"I can't pursue this. Seth's grandfather and others will suffer."

"Have you spoken to him about your concerns?"

"Not really." Imogene slowed dressing.

"You should talk to him."

"What good will it do?"

"He might need to discuss matters. Don't you owe him that little? The man's done much for you."

"True," she replied, knowing only one case which verified Maude's disclosure. "But nothing will come of it."

"Conversation should help. If not you, perhaps him."

Her friend's pleading tone prompted Imogene to resume dressing and honor Seth's request.

"He has asked for you."

"I can't see him alone," she said, being both reluctant and eager for his presence.

"I'll go with you."

Properly outfitted, she and Maude began their journey, arriving at the mansion in short time.

"Thank you for coming, Imogene," Seth said, materializing from opened doors. He nodded greeting to Maude and showed them to a cozy, dim parlor.

Seth's stiff formality pained. After intimacies they'd shared, she wasn't surprised at her feelings nor his demeanor. But it still hurt.

Taking one of the two seats indicated, Imogene observed Maude continue standing and Seth, seemingly unaware of her companion, sit in an adjacent leather chair.

"I must follow through and take Johnetta for my wife," Seth said sadly.

"I know," Imogene barely uttered. Feeling exposed, she regretted coming and saw little need for explanation. He would wed Johnetta and, therefore, be lost to her forever.

A knock and someone entered. "He's here."

"I forgot my appointment with Mr. Johnson," Seth stood. "Please excuse me, ladies." He exited with Frank following.

Eyeing Maude, Imogene stood. "I shouldn't have come." She approached the door.

"You can't go, Immie," her companion said, obviously upset.

"Mr. Johnson's here, in this same house. It's awkward."

"You haven't given Seth chance to talk and explain."

"What can he say that will change anything?"

"You never know. Time can alter things."

She would wait awhile. Easing mounting pressures, she paced across the thick carpet. Steps kept time with the clock's steady ticking and fast beating of her heart.

Seconds passed. Minutes accumulated into hours. Imogene could stand it no longer. She must leave. Adjusting the lace shawl and tiny mob-cap, surrounded by a white velvet bow, she advanced toward the door. Wondering if she should leave Maude asleep upon the sofa, Imogene peeked into the hall.

"What I've waited for these years will soon happen," Recognizing Mr. Johnson's voice, Imogene listened, but feelings of betrayal made her stay out of sight.

"The Thomas and Johnson family will finally be united."

"Yes," she heard Seth reply. Finality in his deep voice conjured sympathy and regrets.

She heard doors opening, felt cool breezes and papers fluttering.

"What's this?" Seth asked.

"The receipt," Mr. Johnson responded.

"For what?"

"You've forgotten. It has been awhile. The old man, Bill Washington, his funeral charges you paid."

Stunned at this discovery, Imogene felt, again, unappreciative and wished things could have been otherwise.

The man she'd once loathed had given much, not asking for anything in return.

"Goodnight, Mr. Johnson," she heard Seth say. Doors closed.

Exposing herself, she said, "I should leave."

"We haven't talked yet." Disappointment was stamped upon his handsome face.

"What good will it do?"

"Perhaps, give some comfort," he said, leading her away from the room where Maude slept.

"Talk with me this night for the last time."

She let him, by gentle touch, secret her away. Her actions were justified by all he'd done for her, and recent knowledge that he'd paid Father's funeral expenses. Staying with this man; being his comfort for this one night was the least she could do. If only, they had a lifetime together.

"I'll stay, Seth," she whispered.

"Thank you, my love," he sighed, pulling her upon the sofa where two forms became one. And night slowly merged into day.

***

Awakening, she felt the urge to leave. But moving from his sleeping form, Imogene felt this final separation, too much like a kind of death and stayed wrapped in his arms. Fully clothed, they had conversed little and caressed much. Sleep had come, saving her from more involvement.

"Rest, my love," Seth had said, releasing her from further obligation other than staying the night with him.

"You didn't slip away," she heard him whisper against her forehead.

Looking upward into his face—thin fuzz had grown around his sensual lips. "Should I have?"

"You tell me. You ran before."

Knocking intercepted her comment, and Frank called from behind closed doors. "It's time."

"Give me a few minutes," Seth replied. He never took his eyes from her and stood, tenderly bringing her with him. "If only, we had more time." He mingled words with kisses, keeping her flushed to his body. Suddenly, too soon, he pushed her at arms length and said, "Duty calls." He seemed unable to continue. "I'll be away until the day of the ceremony."

His words brought back their sad position. Breaking from his touch, she sought shawl and mop-cap. "I must go."

"Frank will drive you home." He came closer and adjusted the shawl about her shoulders. Staying behind, he whispered into her ear, "Grant me one more wish?"

Afraid he wanted love, she didn't speak. Could she in good conscience comply?

Responding, again, to what she hadn't spoken, he said, "Heaven knows I need you in a physical way." Looking almost amused he said sadly, "I had opportunity last night." Turning her to face him, he added, "Imogene, my love—that you will always be if I'm married or not—I ask one thing. Never keep your friendship from me."

She sighed in relief. "That I'll gladly give."

"You promise to grace me with your presence occasionally?"

"We can be friends," she admitted. "But all our meetings must be chaperoned."

"My ever vigilant love," he replied affectionately.

"Seth, are you coming?" Frank called.

"Yes, "He replied, releasing her only after planting kisses across her face. Walking away, he turned and whispered, "If we had more time, I would make love to you incessantly."

'It's late," Frank's voice seethe with rage and impatience.

As her first and only lover disappeared, despair bombarded, making her feel forsaken and alone.

"Are you ready?"

Turning, she realized Frank waited for her. Ignoring the hate in his eyes, she sailed past.

"Your friend left last night."

"Oh! I had forgotten about Maude." Why did this man make her feel stupid and mean? She considered walking, but they hadn't far to travel.

He boarded the carriage first, not offering any assist.

Silence prevailed until they arrived at the destination.

"You've disrupted his life."

Torn between recent pleasantries she'd just enjoyed with Seth and unwanted companionship with Frank, Imogene returned his blistering looks with cold silence.

"Before you, Seth accepted marriage with Johnetta." Frank paused, returning her icy scrutiny.

Seeing no need for response, she gave none. The wedding ceremony had not been postponed. What was this man's complaint?

"Do him a service and stay away!" he spat. A scowl marred his already nasty expression.

Unassisted, she dismounted and turned to leave. Thinking better of leaving without explanations, she stopped and faced him. "I mean Seth no harm. I did at first, but not now. I'll certainly do my part in not hurting him further." Her eyes bored through Frank's lean, pale features. "Mr. Kossel," she said, after mounting steps, entering the house and turning. Her words rung out. "And what're you doing to ease your friend's burdens?" Neither wanting nor expecting an answer, Imogene slammed the door behind.

CHAPTER 14

"Still here, partner?" Frank called from nearby.

"Just leaving," Seth replied. He'd tended his toilet, dressing for travel in Sack suit, high riding boots, shirt and narrow neckwear. Reaching for his bowler, he observed his ally, approaching.

"You seem recovered from earlier."

"Appearances are often deceiving." He placed the hat upon his trimmed head and ran a hand across his clean-shaven face.

"Then you're still bothered?"

"Correct." Seth reached for his small valise that held changing clothes and other necessities for the few days stay. "But, we know, this marriage will happen ... regardless."

"Glad you've accepted that." Frank followed him to the outside exit and stopped, hindering Seth's departure. "Shouldn't be too hard bedding Johnetta and substituting the other woman's image. Won't that compensate?"

"Not in a thousand years." Seth eyed his slender pal. He laughed scornfully. "Way I'm feeling, the marriage will never consummate."

"You're joking?"

Stepping outside, he stopped, turned and said, "Frank, I don't know how to make you understand my dilemma. But it's like the passion you have for wealth, security and virgins. It's equal to giving a man, having tasted only the finest culinary delights upon costly china, a cracked bowl of unseasoned beans and stale bread."

"Oh," Frank mumbled. The look in his eyes gave evidence he understood. "I never realized the hopelessness of your position." His Stetson-hatted head shook. "You would give up pleasures with untried Johnetta for memories of Imogene." His voice held acceptance, but sounded disbelieving.

"When only one woman will or can satisfy, how else can I feel?" He half smiled. "Look, friend, I must go. It's late. Save your ear for later, after the ceremony. I'll need it then. Imogene will only give so much." He rushed down stone steps, secured his bundle and mounted his horse. "Later, friend, he called, beginning the short business journey.

***

Time that should have rushed by loitered like an uninvited, disagreeable guest. Preparing and practicing upcoming speeches, saved Imogene's sanity. But that worked only during day and early evening. When lights turned off and most slept, grief reappeared. She tossed and shifted till sleep came. And, even in slumber longing for her one-time lover returned to haunt.

Seth occupied every dream. His image seeped into each unconsciousness, and she would awake in an agitated state. After his marriage, she prayed this turbulence might lessen. It would never end. How could it? She loved him for always.

***

Church bells rung in the faithful day. Imogene, usually up at this hour, lay swaddled, despite warm breezes from an opened window, in thick covers. She couldn't cease shuddering, this morn. Her teeth clattered, sounding like displaced pebbles.

This must stop! She couldn't just become immobile because Seth and Johnetta were to wed this day. Flinging sheet and blankets aside, she jumped from the bed. Objects started swirling—she must have risen too suddenly. By force of will and clinging to a bedpost, she remained upright. Slowly balance returned, and she began dressing, putting most effort into shutting out the approaching ceremony at noon.

Once attired in personal underthings, flowered day dress and black slippers, Imogene tidied her room. Prompted by a still woozy stomach, she remembered not having eaten since yesterday morning. Breakfast smells of coffee, eggs and bacon further announced morning's meal. She hastened from her rooms and rushed down the hall.

"Good morning, Imogene," the landlady greeted. "Missed you at supper last evening." She wiped her hands upon the red checked apron tied around her corseted, still wide waist.

"I must stop overlooking mealtime." She recalled the dizzy spell experienced earlier. "It's not healthy."

"Most surely," the landlady replied, directing her to a table set with necessities. "Sit. I'll bring tea."

After filling her plate, Imogene speared bits of scrambled eggs and forked the aromatic substance into her mouth. No sooner had she chewed and swallowed the foodstuff, bells tolled in the noon hour. Her stomach rotated and nearly spilled its contents as a piece of bacon slipped from her fingers.

"Are you ill, Imogene?" the landlady asked, approaching. Motherly concern unveiled upon the woman's round face and her brown hand clasped Imogene's unsteady ones. "Water should help."

"No," Imogene whispered, warding off the woman's offer. "The bells reminded me of something—"

"They're only announcing Seth Thomas and Johnetta Johnson's nuptials."

"I know," she barely uttered, regretting mention of the only man she'd allowed close enough to love. And, at this very moment, she would never again permit him that pleasure.

Hours passed in which, at the landlady's insistence, Imogene managed to consume most of her breakfast. They remained at the table and talked of everything and nothing special.

Noise and women voices echoed from the hall. Two fellow roomers appeared, and one, Victoria, exclaimed, "We've had some adventure at the church!"

Hearing the animated roomer, Imogene realized the women must have attended Seth and Johnetta's nuptials.

"Must have been a grand affair," the landlady commented.

"Grand isn't the right word," the second roomer, Bernice, snickered jokingly.

Something about these women's behavior and tone did not seem quite right for having just returned from a sacred and important affair. But before she inquired, knocking sounded. Jumping up; believing Maude came with news, Imogene rushed to the door. Behind her the women babbled on. Before giving full access to the knocker, she peeked through the small opening.

"Have a message for Miss Washington." The speaker was a young male seen about the city running errands for a fee.

"Yes, Lester," she said, granting him entry.

He thrust a folded paper into her hand. "Mr. Seth Thomas sent this." Gone in a flash, the boy darted down Second Avenue.

Warm breezes fluttered the note between her fingers, hastening its opening. Anxiety gripped as she scanned scribbled words which requested her presence at the mansion.

What did he need her for? He had a wife now. Would or, more importantly, should she go?

Finding no justification for honoring his request, she returned to the privacy of her rooms for reflection. She gave minor heed to women's chatter that circulated from the dinning area. Time was needed before making any decisions.

Hours had gone and spread gray casts over the room when, fully dressed, Imogene laid across her bed. Visions floated in her head of Seth and his bride together, alone. Thoughts of him with another woman, even if that female was his wife, were too painful and made Imogene rise from what should have been an ideal resting place. She started pacing carpeted floors; her mind teemed with unanswered questions.

Why had Seth requested her presence? And why ask her to the place where his wife was or should have been? Something was amiss, and she must discover what.

Throwing a flowered shawl across her tousled curls and straightened shoulders, she ventured outside. Night's cool breezes made her pull the wrap closer as she boarded the box buggy and drove away. At her destination, it seemed, in the tick of a second, she had had little time considering possible consequences of her action. What if he were abed with his bride?

The mansion, luminous as day, dispelled former concern. Parted drapes revealed illumination from every window. Doors opened just as she dismounted. Seth had seen her and waited at the entrance. Her steps quickened past a ribbon and flower decorated carriage—the wedding vehicle. She stepped through the portal.

"Everyone's searching for you."

Confused, Imogene stood before Ola, speechless. Why would everyone look for her?

"Oh! I thought you were Johnetta." The maid stepped aside, allowing additional access.

Totally baffled now, she paused and looked inside, asking, "Is Seth here?" So as not to appear brazen since he had married, she quickly added, "He sent for me."

"Come in," the stern-looking woman insisted, widening the passage even more. Oddly, the older woman was dressed in silk lace and not in her usual black and white.

She instantly complied and awaited Ola's further directive.

"He was here earlier. But he's gone now."

"Oh," she nearly moaned, believing he'd gone on honeymoon." And, once again, feeling misplaced, she turned. "I'll not stay."

"We don't plan on bedding down until he returns." The older woman urged her into the study. "Ben's still up. He's asked for you."

Following Ola, she beheld the elder man in his usual chair. He gave her a startled look at first which soon turned pleased.

"Imogene, what a pleasant surprise." His arms opened. "Come, child."

"Forgive me for staying away," she apologized, hurrying into his welcoming embrace. Relationship with the older man, somehow, eased the loss of her father. After planting a kiss upon the senior's bald spot, she sat upon cushions at his slippered feet. Noticing he was also dressed in evening garb and wanting answers, she casually stated, "It was a beautiful day for the wedding."

"Yes, had there been one," he replied matter-of-factly.

Queries really overflowed at his statement. She looked from Ben to Ola, hoping for explanations. None came. The old man stared into burning embers in the fireplace, and Ola seemed more occupied with mending spread across her spacious lap. And neither appeared to notice Imogene's questioning gaze.

"I'm back," a welcome voice said.

Imogene looked up and saw Seth approaching. She stood, eager for his greeting. But he walked pass and stood near the burning hearth. And she admired how the fire's glow highlighted his magnificent form.

"We found neither one," Seth said, facing them. His dark eyes spanned the room, falling upon Ola and his grandfather, avoiding her.

Imogene continued standing. She felt like an interference, an unwanted intruder. And when he finally noticed her, the silent examination he gave from head to toe chilled, making her want to run and hide.

"Both vanishings might be connected," the older male said.

"They were seen together last," Seth replied. "Mr. Johnson has hired a private detective for continuing search."

"Seem there's nothing to be done now." Leaving her sewing, Ola stood. "Seth, help me put Ben to bed."

All three exited, not saying a word to Imogene. She held no hard feelings toward the two elders. They had acknowledged her presence—totally unlike indifference Seth had shown. He had some nerve! Hadn't he requested her appearance? Well, she didn't have to stay. Righting the bonnet over her unruly hair and anchoring the shawl about her person, she marched out the library and hastened toward outside doors.

"Running away? How typical of you."

Looking up; facing her mocker, she, with surprised anger, cried, "Oh! You requested my presence and wholly ignored me when I comply!" An urge came over her to pound upon his chest in hopes of relieving growing hurt and rage. But, keeping control, her balled fists stayed still.

"Why didn't you come earlier?" Not waiting for any reply, he continued with, "Evidently your promise of friendship meant nothing!"

"Seth," she pleaded, fight leaving her. She didn't want wrath only his love. "Your wife—the wedding. It was too soon."

"You don't know?" His voice had turned less harsh.

"Know what?"

"Imogene, there was no wedding. Johnetta never arrived at the church."

Both startled and relieved, she nearly fell into his arms, but asked instead, "Why would she have missed an occasion she lauded and prayed for?"

"Can't imagine why." He gathered her close and rested his chin upon her head. "We had some silly disagreement. But that's not unusual." He removed her bonnet and shawl, tossing them upon a coat rack. "We have been given more time, love."

Letting herself savor his warmth and strength, Imogene wrapped her arms around his taunt middle and quieted guilt feelings. Johnetta's disappearance in no way released him from the vow. Only the girl's death—God forbid—would do that. "Surely she'll return. And when she does—"

"Don't destroy our joy," he pleaded, whispering against her skin. "She's not here and not my wife yet," he asserted. "Stay with me tonight, love."

Resulting moisture and heat weakened her defenses. She wavered. Being together again would only prolong heartache, making it even harder to part. But if some providence gave them another chance to love, why deny herself?

"Imogene?"

"Yes, yes," she answered, sensing his incomplete request.

He led her by the hand into private quarters. They entered an area she had never seen before. The rose draped room gave off exotic smells like burning incense. Outfitted with small armless sofa and cushions that circled a large fireplace. A glass enclosed cabinet overflowed with books. Imogene suspected Seth used this place as his private domain, his sanctuary.

"Come, Imogene," he whispered, pulling her with him upon the cushions. "Here, love." He urged her upon his lap and began kissing her face, wayward curls and down her clothed bosom.

When, at last, she recovered somewhat from his onslaught, she rested upon his shoulder. Things were moving so fast. They had only made love once, and she felt slight shyness at the actuality of intimacy with him again. She suspected he had sensed that apprehension when he released, slid her from his lap and stretched out upon the floor pillows, saying, "There's no rush. We have this night and more, perhaps."

No longer feeling any urgency, she found herself relaxing. And when he patted the place by his side, she laid there.

"I know so little about you. Tell me everything, your hopes and fears. I'll need these memories, my love, when —"

"—you marry," she completed for him. Reminded, once again, they had, for certain, the moment, her story began. She told him about earlier, happier times when material and emotional well-being were hers and, most importantly, when she had family.

Soothing him with reassurances, as his handsome features clouded with regrets, that she knew now he had never been responsible for her father's death and thanked him for paying burial expenses that were, rightly, hers.

"I felt, somehow, responsible for you, my love—a woman alone," he responded. Lifting up, he planted a kiss upon her forehead.

"How fortunate, though denying it, I was." Instinctively, she returned his affection, snuggling close. "And I'm still favored to have this moment; your love."

"For now and always," he asserted, pulling her even closer. After long silence, he continued saying, "You know I, because of others, must wed. But you'll always possess my heart."

Forcing back tears for what she could have had as this man's wife, Imogene listened while he related his life's story.

He talked about adventures as a youth, relationships with family and the cursed promise made between the Thomas and

Johnson households. They conversed, much as friends would have, sharing laughs and sorrows well into the night, the inevitable happened. Speech ceased and touch began.

He lifted her like a feather, laying her atop him. Ifs, whats and might have beens no longer mattered. Their bodies, lips and breaths melded. Their desires were one and the same: consummation.

Taking each clue, what he did to her she did to him. Every kiss he gave, invading her mouth and capturing her tongue with his, she copied. When he traced kisses across her face, down her neck and loosened her bodice to rain them upon her exposed bosom, she did not falter, but undid his shirt and showered his hard chest with like caresses. Momentarily they stilled and completely disrobed one another.

Seth and Imogene stood naked, swaying flesh to flesh. In silent gratification or, more accurately, adoration, they savored the moment. This must last both their lifetimes.

But love can be denied only so long. It must flourish.

Conjointly they returned to rumpled cushions, disconnecting only long enough for her relaxing and his crouching above. Their lips met simultaneously while she prepared for their second matting. She wondered if this would be as before when Seth positioned between her limbs.

"Don't fear, love," he whispered, touching secret places.

"Seth," she softly moaned.

"Open, my love," he instructed, entering her.

Words lodged in her throat as she melded with his rigidity, and he took the lead, taking her to a place she had been before. But soon realizing where he'd taken her, though similar to the first time, was vastly different now. All reasoning left as Seth directed by movement and touch. Only the seconds, minutes, what seemed hours, mattered and that they hold nothing from each other. Believing Seth, her first and only lover, would cement their bond, she matched his thrusts until they both succumbed, yielding all. At last, their matting culminated. Seth and Imogene relaxed with moist arms and legs entwined.

***

"Where are you?" Imogene rubbed sleep from her eyes.
"They found her." The male voice, not Seth's, sounded far.

CHAPTER 15

"Holy Mary!" Seth muttered, concealing Imogene's nakedness with some flowered shawl that laid nearby. "Coming!" he called, donning only his trousers.

"Where are you going?" The woman he loved had awakened.

"Can't explain now, my love," he whispered, leaving and securing the door behind.

"Took long enough," someone mumbled.

Ola stood in his line of vision, but she had not spoken.

"Yes. Johnetta's back." Frank seemed tipsy, besotted and unlike his usual smug self.

"And so have you," he remarked, referring to Frank. "You took the missing bride home." No ceremony would be performed at this hour anyway. Besides, another occupied his thoughts.

"You're not concerned with Johnetta?" Ola asked, looking down the hall. "She's here."

"Here?" He remembered his state of undress, and, more importantly, he recalled Imogene's presence. "Nothing can be done now. Take the girl home!"

"How cold," Frank mocked. Looking toward Seth's private reading room, he asked, "Who's in there? Has another taken Johnetta's place?"

"Give me a minute." He turned where Imogene waited. "I'll dress and take Johnetta home."

"Aren't you curious why and where she's been?"

"Should I be?" he replied, only anxious about Imogene.

"I'll go to the child," Ola said, hurrying away.

"We need to talk, Seth."

He eyed the man impatiently and waited.

"Not here," Frank said, walking ahead to the reading room.

"No!" he shouted, blocking his partner's advance.

"What trollop you hiding in there?" Frank demanded.

"Speak what you know," he answered angrily and directed Frank to another room.

"Who is it?"

"That's none of your business."

"Imogene," Frank asserted like some victor.

"What do you want to discuss?" He'd lost patience and resented being kept from the woman he'd made love to.

"Need a drink." Frank reached for the decanter and poured himself a generous portion. He took several swallows before saying, "I've been with your intended the whole time."

"Complaining about me again?" Seth knew his partner always gave Johnetta a ready ear. Often Frank had told him of such conversations, as if he might change Seth's indifferent treatment of the girl. But he always welcomed his friend's interference. It relieved him of being bothered. After their wedding, was soon enough to be saddled with Johnetta.

"That and—" Taking another drink, Frank continued saying, "—other things."

Seth continued standing near the exit. He felt an urgency. Imogene might need reassurance.

"Tell me, friend, what would you do if—" Frank seemed unable to continue just as the door flew open.

"Frank, where are you? I didn't want to come here in the first place!" Johnetta appeared. The yellow flowers upon her bonnet swayed as she rushed past Seth and confronted his, uncommonly paler associate.

"Someone should take her home immediately," Ola said, joining them.

Frank looked at Seth.

Seth returned his partner's stare.

Johnetta's slight form snapped around. She appeared, for the first time, aware of Seth. After surveying his state of undress, her youthful features turned haughty, and she said, After our last argument, I have nothing to say to you." Latching upon Frank's forearm, she commanded, "Take me home!"

"We can talk later," Seth said, removing the empty glass from his partner's hand. He deposited the container upon the table. Exiting he said, "Best do as she says, pal."

With one woman in mind, he advanced to his private reading room and searched the enclosed area. Not seeing her, the only woman he'd ever wanted, a sense of dread fell upon him.

"Seth?"

"It's me," he replied, moving where she stood, completely dressed. "I feared you'd run away again."

"No," she seemed to sigh, putting distance between them. "What has happened?" Her hazel eyes held his. Fear seemed to peek from their depths.

"Come, Imogene." With outstretched hands, he urged her where he sat upon the bed. "She's returned," he confessed.

"I know." She exhaled, not hindering him pulling her closer nor stopping him from sandwiching her hands within his.

"If only, things could be different." He wished with all his heart Grandfather and Ola were not involved. It mattered little to him about loss of property and wealth. He could go elsewhere and start over with Imogene at his side. And Frank, from their earlier exploits, had proven himself a born survivor.

"Can't be helped," she replied, her voice full of lament. "I should leave." She attempted standing.

"No," he pleaded, pressing her to sit. "Why shouldn't we take full advantage of this time?"

Not responding, but moving closer, she nestled into his body, and two forms became one. Neither spoke of the anguish prevalent in their hearts. The only concern for both, to savor this moment.

***

"Is it possible?" Imogene asked. "Johnetta always praised Seth and couldn't wait for the wedding."

"I saw the announcement in the Chronicle shortly after her return," Maude said matter-of-factly. She appeared more interested with papers scattered upon the desk.

"Why was the ceremony postponed?" Imogene rose from her favorite chair and ambled toward the opened window. Her eyes peered through its sheer motionless hangings, which indicated promises of a hot, sticky day. "I can't imagine why they aren't wed," she said more to herself than to Maude.

"Imogene, you of all people, should know that answer," "Why?" She turned and saw Maude had pushed aside papers.

"And why not you?" Her stately form stood. "Considering your relationship with Seth Thomas—"

"What do you mean!" Anger overtook her. "I have not seen him since Johnetta's return!"

"Oh, and why not?" Maude seemed totally unaffected with any show of hostility. She returned to her papers.

"I'm no hoyden! I can't keep interfering with his and her relationship."

"Open your eyes, Imogene," Maude said calmly. "Their whole affair has been wrong, and since Johnetta's return, she's had nothing to do with him."

Imogene, totally confused, stood dumfounded.

"This was told me by reliable sources."

Additional questions budded in her mind, she could not picture herself asking Johnetta anything personal. But Seth would honestly, she believed, answer her queries. She had vowed not to be alone with him since the last time. They could never make love again. It was so painful adjusting afterwards to what would never result in marriage. He was promised to another.

"I'll return." Maude had pushed from the desk and exited.

Having no idea what her friend was about, Imogene waited. Anxiety burdened her heart and weighted her feet as she paced the multicolored carpet.

"Hello, Imogene."

Swirling around quickly and stopping, she felt the gentle swaying of her skirts. Speechless, she observed the man who had gradually occupied dreams and thoughts and now he had become too much a part of her life. Her eyes traveled the breath and length of him, clean shaven; attired in dark Sack suit and boots.

"You're a heartless creature, avoiding me for the past weeks," he seemed to scold in a teasing manner.

"I—" Words deserted. Yes, she had hid from him, often going extra distance to avoid his home and places, she knew. he frequented. Her heart began booming as he approached like some predatory animal in quest of nourishment.

"I didn't see your buggy out front." He stood within touch.

"I walked," she replied, not telling him only exercise, as of late, helped her concentration upon daily tasks.

"It does clear the head," A half-smiled played over his lips. A breath away from her now, he whispered, "I've missed you, my love."

"Don't call me that!" She pulled from his touch. "You are still to be wed."

"Unfortunately that's probably true, even though Johnetta has postponed the event indefinitely and won't talk or see me. Needless to say, the Johnsons are livid. She won't give explanation for her actions.

Glad Seth kept his distance, she moved even further away. Standing near the hearth, unlit and barren—so like the way she felt—Imogene did not speak. Her mind, befuddled with the whole situation, focused upon the man before her, Seth Thomas. How did I ever let him, of all men, get this close? she wondered.

"I've appraised my position and see no way out of the promise made by my family and the Johnsons."

"True." His words forced her to continue saying, "That's why we must end our relationship."

"Going back on your word?" He, upon her in seconds, said with confrontation, "You promised friendship!"

"But, Seth—" What kept her in his grasp? Not admitting why, she continued speaking. "—when we're together, things happen, and intimacy results."

"We are still unmarried, consenting adults?"

By now Imogene, mesmerized by Seth's nearness, his very presence and memories they had shared, would not move from his arms. Welcoming and returning her lover's kisses, she rejected inhibitions. Nearly loss in the moment, she heard knocking. The tapping, it seemed, sounded from a great distance. When Seth had stepped away, leaving her alone, did she become fully aware.

"Mr. Johnson's arrived," Maude said.

"I must go." One would have thought he only spoke to Imogene because Seth's dark eyes stayed upon her. "We'll talk later," he said with certainty, ambling away.

"Well, how did it go?" Maude asked.

"Nothing's solved," she confessed.

"That wasn't my aim. You seemed to need his presence. You've alluded to him our entire conversation."

"I—I didn't realize."

"Want to talk? This can wait," Maude said, pushing papers away and resuming her seat.

"How can he have become such an obsession? I detested him before, but now I feel incomplete when he's absent." She remained standing with her arms clasped.

"Sounds like love," Maude said reflectively.

"I'm glad, for purely selfish reasons, the wedding's delayed." Recalling something else he'd told her, she continued. "And Johnetta won't see Seth. He's not spoken to her since her return. Can you believe it!"

"Might she have another love? Youth is often fickle."

"I never thought of that. But her parents have only allowed Seth to pay her court. I've not known any other man given that privilege."

"Strange ... But does it matter? Imogene. What counts, seems to me, Seth Thomas is still unmarried. All's fair in war and love."

"I'm not certain that's always true, Maude." She recalled evil deeds—one person hurting the other—in love's name.

"If Johnetta's not spoken to him sent her return, one must assume she wants the relationship dissolved and over with."

"But the vow ... Seth's still obligated. Her parent's has the final say so, and they'll not relent. Property and money are involved."

"Immie, there might be more involved in Johnetta's actions than what's on the surface."

"You have proof?" She'd not relaxed since their talk, and now she fell into a favored chair and sighed in hopeful relief.

"It's mostly female intuition."

"Oh." She, dishearten again, sunk deeper into the chair. Perhaps she'd find comfort there. Solace, it appeared, was not to be hers. Besides unanswered queries about Johnetta, Imogene feared another concern. Had his seed taken root from the first time they'd made love? Was she carrying Seth's child?

***

"Not curious why Johnetta keeps avoiding you?"

Seth looked up from financial books and studied his friend. He wondered more why the slender man looked leaner and more ashen than usual.

"I talked to her yesterday. Brought up you and the wedding. She wouldn't discuss either issue." Frank poured a hefty drink and continued standing.

"You're drinking a lot lately. Are you well? A doctor visit or time away might help."

"Johnetta's condition's what matters, not my health. Which is fine!" Frank said too intensely. He bent over, eye-level to Seth's seated figure. "The marriage ceremony should go on."

"Why? This is a reprieve of sorts. Gives me more time with Imogene. After this marriage foolishness, I have needed her even more."

"You don't care Johnetta spent the entire time with me when she should have been at the church?"

"We clashed more than usual the evening before. How often have you told me she sought you out after our disagreements?" Abandoning his bookkeeping, Seth pushed from the desk and stood. This conversation was not to his liking. "What did you want to discuss earlier?"

"Oh!" Frank looked like a cornered rat. He straightened, poured another drink and gulped it down. "Well, your know it's about Johnetta."

He only nodded, growing suspect of his partner's unease. What could have effected his usually complacent friend so?

"Well," Frank said. And after coughing several times, he continued speaking. "Listening to someone's complaints would develop into some kind of closeness. You agree?"

Not responding, Seth waited.

"You know Johnetta's sought me often at prearranged, secret places. She's often cried her poor heart out over you. I gave comfort. I was forced to. The innocent child stirred like no other woman ever had. She's the first pure, clean woman I've ever known."

"You sound like a man smitten."

"Nothing was suppose to happen." Gloom fell over the man. Sweat collected upon his face, and he began pacing. "She needed comfort, and—and I gave it to her."

"That's what you've done all along. Why do I sense this last time was different?" Seth suspected the answer, but he needed confirmation.

Sticking a bony finger inside the collar of his shirt, Frank's Adam's apple moved several times, but words did not come. His whole demeanor changed. He seemed more himself when he said, "You're right. I always gave her a ready ear; nothing less ..."

"This is what you've wanted to discuss?" Something about his partner's tone left doubt. "There's more?"

"Nor anything less," Frank commented, exiting.

Watching his associate hurry down the hall, Seth knew the man wanted to say more. Not worried. Frank would come around and reveal everything. They had no secrets. He knew his friend would not disappoint more surely than he knew if Imogene would keep her promise of continual friendship. Putting aside Frank's masked words; the uncertainty of his pending marriage and the reasons for Johnetta not explaining, Seth returned to his books with one precious object upon his mind: the only woman he'd ever wanted to love, cherish and marry, Imogene.

CHAPTER 16

Buttoning the dark bodice of her over-dress, Imogene pondered. Maude's physician had revealed earlier suspicions and confirmed what would alter her life now and forever.

"Immie, may I come in?"

"Yes," she replied, giving Maude admittance.

"Are you?" Concern played over her friend's dark, dignified features.

"Yes," she admitted, encompassing her slightly swollen middle in both palms.

"When the child's born, Dr. Harper did tell you there are many childless couples willing to adopt—"

"That's out of the question! How can I forsake the product of his and my love? Her arms spread as if they were a fortress around the unborn being inside.

"Well, Seth Thomas, I'm sure, will assist you financially."

"Oh, no! I'll not ask him for anything. And you must not tell him."

"Being the father, he has a right to know."

"I'll not let this influence his decision regarding the wedding."

"Johnetta's refused to see him. How can any relationship proceed under those circumstances?"

"I don't know. But I'll not be implicated in whatever decision he makes."

"Immie, the instant he became attracted and you accepted his love sealed your involvement. How can his judgments be excluded now?"

Momentarily perplexed—much weighed on her mind—Imogene rejected reasoning. She only wanted to be alone.

"No matter," Maude said, clearly taking her unresponsiveness as need for isolation. "Right now rest and quiet are what you need." Her friend and mentor opened the door.

"Why don't you spend the rest of the day with us? I'll have Mother prepare some tea, and we can, if you like later, talk."

When the door closed, Imogene reclined atop the bed in quiet, and it was as if she, cushioned in comfort and warmth, laid within her mother's bosom. Surely worries would slip away. But only temporary peace came. Slumber eluded. Much cluttered her head and heart.

After tossing for several minutes, she abandoned hopes of sleep and began pacing. Thoughts were absorbed with Seth and the life they'd created. Raising their child alone would not be easy, but succeed she would. Money saved from sewing plus smaller amounts earned giving speeches for suffragettism would help. Public banishment, hurtful for herself and mostly the child, might hurt, but she wouldn't let it hamper. And what about her first and only love? Living without Seth the rest of her life, she must survive.

"Immie," someone called from the closed entrance.

"Yes," She gave admittance. "I couldn't sleep."

"Heard you pacing. Mother has a pot of tea ready. It might help." Not waiting for a reply, Maude urged her forward.

Believing nothing would help, Imogene followed her ally. She saw matters only darkening and great strength required.

***

"How long are you going to let this go on, Seth?"

"Only Johnetta can answer that question, Frank. She still communicating with you?" Seth replied.

"Whenever she can slip away. Her father's like a second shadow."

"That reminds me I must speak to Mr. Johnson about the wedding."

"Johnetta's agreed to a date?" Frank's lean features brightened, and he ceased shuffling playing cards.

"I've heard nothing. But my life can't stop until she's ready. Too many weeks have passed. I won't wait any longer!" He shoved his promising poker hand aside and stood. "If only the Johnsons admitted the unfairness and fruitlessness of that damn promise!"

"Hopeless dream," his companion didn't quite sneer.

"Mr. Johnson's here, nephew," Ola called from the foyer.

"Speak of the devil!" Frank appeared agitated. He grabbed the deck of cards, and veins in his claw-like hands appeared to have popped out, like greenish worms. "Why is he here?"

"For me." Seth stressed, noticing his friend's great disquiet. "This might take awhile."

Frank silently shut the door, shrinking from sight.

Seth strolled purposely behind Ola.

"Not too late, I hope, Seth," Mr. Johnson, in his usual black attire, said as Seth entered the library.

"Doesn't matter." He waited while the undertaker tossed his top hat upon a side table and sat. "Your daughter's irrational behavior should indicate the foolishness of keeping this oath neither of us made or wanted."

"Johnetta's never objected before. In fact, she's only expressed favor with the whole affair ... until now." The man shifted his black boots before continuing with, "Can't see what's come over her. Given time, she'll come around."

"That's just it. I want to get on with my life."

"I don't see how this minor problem keeps you—other than getting married—from living your life." The man's intolerance, very evident, suddenly became masked. "We are men with needs. I can understand there being another woman or women of low virtue—"

"There's only one and she's not—" Seth hoped he'd stopped before revealing anything that might harm Imogene.

"Appears those rumors are true. Who is she?"

Sighing, Seth whispered a quiet, "Thanks." The man didn't know the identity of his true love. Dismissing the undertaker's question, he said, "Does it matter?" What did he care about the older man's higher status? Imogene must be protected.

"Yes, if you're thinking of reneging." Johnetta's parent stood, emphasizing, it seemed, his superior position.

"My parents made the damn pledge, not I," he said. Had he let valor overrule common sense?

"Seth, don't make me your enemy." Johnson spoke in a fatherly, mildly threatening manner. "I don't want to destroy you and your family."

For an instant, Seth had viewed a side of the undertaker he'd not noticed before. His future father-in-law always treated him much as a doting uncle would a favorite nephew. And when the older man's menacing face reverted, Seth wondered if he'd been mistaken. But Johnson's final words left no mistake as to his intentions.

"I'll leave now." Snatching up his top hat and sliding its black brim between his immaculate, too feminine-looking hands, Johnson stood. "Prepare yourself for the ceremony in two days!"

"I wasn't aware Johnetta's made up her mind." Seth tried shaking anguish and rage slashing him like a sword. But he couldn't and blared, "Why didn't you tell me this earlier?"

"My daughter's still not talking. She will marry you if I have to bind and haul her to the church!" He slapped the top hat upon his dark head, as if for emphasis. "We'll see you at the church two days from now at noon."

"You know your way out," Seth said, remaining seated. Much weighed upon his mind to bother with formality.

"It's settled then." Frank stood at the entrance. Relief shown upon his face, and a smile—not at all mocking—graced his thin lips.

"You wanted to discuss something with me." Seth recalled his friend's earlier concern.

"Not urgent now. Johnetta'll be safely married."

He studied Frank's complacent attitude. Things were amiss. Since his partner's return weeks ago with Johnetta, the man had wavered betwixt smugness and uneasiness.

"Were you and she intimate?" Seth asked what he'd suspected all along.

"I'm not crazy. Even if you don't care, her father would roast me alive for taking that liberty."

Studying his companion's hasty steps to the whiskey bottle, convinced Seth Frank's declarations were false. And when the man raised the glass, drops spilling over the rim, to his lips he was nearly certain.

"Were you?" he repeated.

"Don't matter, friend. She'll be your wife."

"Deflowered by you."

"If you cared, why didn't you bed Johnetta and not pursue Bill's stubborn daughter!"

"In spite of Imogene's age, she'd never had a man before me." He still had proof. The faded spot, after many washings, had stayed imprinted upon the sheets.

Looks akin to surprise, envy or regret danced across his partner's angular features.

"Even if I owned up to it, her father would never relent. Johnetta's destined to marry you."

"What if she's carrying your child, Frank? Could you accept that?"

"Could you?" his companion retorted, obviously upset. Then realizing something, he quickly added, "I've admitted nothing."

Seth laughed, not at all amused. He said, "Friend, you've answered my suspicions and only added to my woes. "What were you thinking? Is anything solved?"

"She was too willing, crying on my shoulder about your indifference toward her. I never meant to—"

"I care less that you eased Johnetta's distress or made love to her. She never appealed to me, and through no fault of hers, I resented the child even more because I must wed her." He held onto Frank's wavering gaze. "What hurts, my bosom buddy, is you've done no one any good: Johnetta, yourself or me. After the marriage, how can you and she openly express any feelings? And the child ..."

"I don't know that she's carrying my baby!" Frank shouted. Then his voice softened. "I never meant any harm to her or you.

We were together and things happened. I only tried to ease your troubles."

Seth laughed mockingly. "You wanted to ease my woes. Friend, weren't there more efficient, less destructive ways?"

Hurt displayed in Frank's eyes conveyed, more than words, the man's apology.

Seth sighed. Things could get no worse. Not only did he feel division between his and Frank's long friendship, but, Imogene. The fragile bond between them, now, no doubt, might permanently diminish and die.

Frank, visibly shaken and repentant, discarded his nearly full drink and left silently.

In two days when legally united to a female other than the woman he loved, Imogene, he would be like a dead person existing. Should loveless existence be termed anything but?

***

"Ceremony's this morning."

Imogene turned at Maude's announcement. But from sick sensations stirring in her belly, she quickly grabbed her quivering stomach.

"Immie, are you all right?" Maude rushed to her side. "I should have said nothing."

"No, I'm glad you did. This will stop my foolish hopes. Seth and I can never be." She stood, reaching for her shawl and bonnet. "We'll be late for the assembly."

"Perhaps, I should go in your place. The meeting's in the church where the nuptials will be."

"No. This is just another feat I must overcome," she declared with more conviction than she actually felt.

Arriving at their destination in fast time, Imogene pulled up just as an enclosed buggy stopped behind. Rushing ahead, she paid scant attention to the carriage or its occupants and entered the full assembly room. Before she approached the podium, someone pulled at her elbow.

"We just made it, Immie."

"What?" she replied, moderately slowing her pace.

"The wedding party had pulled up behind us."

"Oh," she mumbled, hoping she sounded untroubled and thankful Maude hadn't time to say more.

"Everyone, our distinguished speaker and fellow suffragist has arrived," a female commentator called.

Imogene positioned behind the podium; thanked all for their attendance and forged into her speech. Like always, she became absorbed in the message and, for awhile, forgot the nuptial service in the chapel. And at the end of her talk, she, not gathering with others for small talk, tea or cookies, rushed away—Maude had elected to remain and would ride with another.

Sanctuary doors were ajar, and organ music played softly in the background. Ignoring all reasons for not observing happenings inside, she peeked at the majestic interior and scanned the backs of four persons occupying the front row.

"Do you take this woman to be your wife, to have and to hold in sickness and in health till death do you part?"

Imogene's eyes passed from Rev. Morris to an imposing figure just addressed. Recognizing Seth as the appealing person in black and white finery, her gaze stayed on him.

"Mr. Thomas, did you hear?" the minister said. "Do you take this woman as wife?"

When Seth's response faltered, a tall, lean figure stood in the congregation, not speaking.

Seth's handsome visage shifted from the reverend's composed features to the standing man who Imogene saw was Mr. Johnson.

"Do you, Seth Thomas, take Johnetta Marla Johnson as your wife?" the pastor asked again.

All turned toward the groom as Imogene had and awaited the expected response. Praying the father of her unborn child would somehow decline, knots formed in her womb as silence grew.

"I do," resounded throughout the church.

His answer must be yes, but still feeling betrayed, she clutched her aching middle and departed the scene.

CHAPTER 17

She stood just outside the church. Cool breezes neither refreshed nor delighted. Imogene's mind, congested with loss, found relief in nothing. Seth, now married, had sealed her fate. She must birth and raise their child alone—never would she let another man this close ... ever again.

"Immie, you still here?" Maude approached with two other women recognized from the earlier meeting.

"Can we talk?" Imogene said, nodding acknowledgment to the other females. "It's urgent."

"Of course," Imogene heard Maude say from behind as she boarded the box buggy and waved to former companions.

"He's married now," she said, maneuvering her buggy down congested streets. "It's best I leave town. Seth must never suspect I'm carrying his child." One hand wiped a tear slipping down her cheek.

"Immie, watch out!" Maude screamed, saving them from colliding with another vehicle.

"Cursed woman!" the other driver, a bushy-bearded oldster, spat, never slowing his barrel-laden wagon.

The scream stuck in her throat as she forced back further tears. "Can't stay here."

Maude offered no objections as their journey continued in silence. She only clasped her shoulder in assurance.

***

"I do," Seth had heard himself say even though his whole being had cried out, "No!"

What choice had he?

None, he knew as his eyes beheld Grandfather and Ola.

"—do you, Johnetta Johnson, take this man, Seth Thomas, as your husband?" the preacher said, drawing everyone's heed.

Quiet prevailed as all followed Seth's examination of his soon-to-be-bride.

No reply came. Johnetta, adorned in white silk and lace from head to toe, avoided every eye. She snatched her tiny gloved hands from his.

"Did you hear, Johnetta, my child?" the pastor asked.

She clutched fingers, hiding the gold wedding ring upon her finger, saying nothing.

Would she might refuse, releasing him again? Seth waited patiently and hoped she couldn't find words.

"Child—" the minister pleaded. "Ans—"

"Answer him!" Mr. Johnson squawked. Voice and black-suited form made him resemble some tormenting crow. The man started toward his sibling. He only returned to his seat under duress from others.

"Will you take this man to be your spouse." The preacher spoke in coaxing tones. When no response came, the man said, "Just answer yes, child."

Still no reply shattered the quiet.

Seth observed Mrs. Johnson doing her best at restraining her husband with touches and whispers. But the slight woman's efforts were short-lived. When the young bride stayed mute and only fumbled with the lace upon her long sleeves, the little woman's spouse tore from her side.

"Daughter, if you don't answer, I'll make all my threats truths!" Mr. Johnson shouted.

Seth followed every eye to the young woman as her childish features expressed the terror she must have felt.

"Once again," Rev. Morris pleaded. "Will you, young lady, take this man for your husband?"

"I—I—" Her words were reluctant. After her dark eyes darted toward her father, she screeched, "I can't!"

Seth, impatient for an end to this entire affair, doubted she would give any plausible reason for her words.

"Why, child?" Pastor asked, silencing all with lifted hand.

Tears spilled down Johnetta's pale cheeks before she cried out, "Because I'm already married."

Turbulence broke out from everywhere. The mighty chapel walls shook and rumbled, threatening, it seemed, to fall apart. The few people present converged around weeping Johnetta. Even Seth captured her trembling hands, and this unexpected welcomed news didn't stop him from sympathizing with the girl's plight.

"Out my way!" Mr. Johnson, pushing and shoving, broke through the wall of people concealing his daughter. "Who is he, the man you married?"

Only her piercing sobs responded.

"Go home!" The undertaker flung his off-spring toward her mother. "Get out of my sight. And you will identify the man, the fool, who dared wed my daughter." The man turned and urged the minister aside, saying, "We must talk."

Stunned, Seth watched Mr. Johnson and Pastor, two figures shrouded in black and huddled close, leave for a private place. Sighing in relief—he could marry Imogene now—Seth approached his grandfather and aunt.

"What man's crazy enough to marry that child. Everybody knows she's promised to you." Ola said, shaking her flower-bonneted head.

"A fitting end for what should have never been," the elder Thomas declared.

Seth nodded, exhaled and said, "Shall we leave?"

"Yes, grandson. I'm tired out with all this unexpected excitement."

Ola rushed ahead, mumbling something not understood. The yellow false blossoms atop her hat seemed near flight with each advance of her wide, swaying body.

Seth lifted Ben's disabled form, once perfectly fit, and followed Ola outside. Once all were in the carriage, he started for home. While on the short journey, Ola's mumbling never ceased, and Ben, settled in his well-padded seat, dozed.

Seth's mind flooded with thoughts of Imogene and what bliss would soon be theirs, He couldn't wait to tell her. With his family safely home, he'd find his lover and announce the good news.

"Nephew, where you goin'?" Ola screamed, diverting his concentration.

The mansion laid behind. Quickly turning and backtracking, he stopped before their destination. Ola dismounted, ignoring or not noticing his offer of help. He lifted Ben's sleeping shape—Ben never stirred—and mounted stairs to their home.

"Where's your wife, Johnetta?" Frank stood at the door.

"You won't believe what occurred," Seth said, striding toward Ben's bed room. "Let me see to grandfather first."

"Lay him down." Ola had covers already pulled back. "I'll see to Ben. If I need you, I'll call."

Leaving, he saw Frank prancing in the hall. "Johnetta's already married."

Why did his partner not seem surprised or, at least, irate? The man had been intimate with her. Frank only seemed wired up, like rubber pulled too taunt and near bursting.

"She name the man?"

"No, Frank, she didn't."

Relief poured over his friend's face.

"But I pity Johnetta. Her father's fit to be tied. When he gets home and confronts—"

"Where is she?" Frank shouted.

"She and her mother left for home. Mr. Johnson stayed with the pastor."

"Talk to you later!" Frank said, He was gone in seconds.

What caused his partner's hasty departure. And since Johnetta was a married woman now, Frank wouldn't have further involvement with her, least, not openly. Unless—

"Seth," he heard Ola call.

"Coming," he replied. Putting aside summations.

"Sit," Ben said, patting the bed. Grandfather's wide lips smiled. "It's finally over with."

Seth nodded.

"Don't delay. Go to her."

He knew what Ben meant. Hadn't he told the senior enough of his love for Imogene?

"Now the way's clear, Don't allow anything else to come between you two. Go to her!"

After giving Ben a hug, Seth left. Outside and mounted, he, not certain where Imogene might be, raced toward Maude's residence. There in short time, he saw a stately woman going inside the home. Thinking she Imogene, he called her name.

"Seth." The woman, Maude, had turned and came near. "Imogene's not here I haven't long left her."

"Where?" he asked, staying mounted.

"She's going home." Maude appeared unsure when she said, "I doubt she's still there."

"Why?" His horse began prancing impatiently, mirroring frustrations he felt. "I must speak to her." Seeing Maude's continued reluctance, he said, "There was no marriage."

"Goodness!" Shock registered upon the female's refined features. Her slender fingers played with her silk bodice. "She needn't have gone."

"Where is she?" He neither soften his voice nor apologized for its harshness. "Tell me!"

"I promised not to. But things are different. She's going to a home managed by friends. It's no more than an hour's ride. If you leave now, perhaps—"

"Give me the directions," he said interrupting.

Maude quickly complied, wished him well and waved, smiling encouragement, as he sprinted away.

"Seth!" came from afar.

He looked and saw Frank approaching. Slowing, he said, "Not now. There's urgent business."

"Mine's a matter of life and death."

Could he forsake his friend? He knew where Imogene had gone and would continue the journey afterwards. They had a lifetime for sharing and loving now. He waited for his partner.

"I need my share of our available assets."

"You're dissolving our partnership?"

"Must get away. I'll be, if you want, an absent ally."

"What brought this on?" Seth suspected Johnetta, somehow, involved. But he couldn't imagine how with her being married to another.

"Not here. Once we get to the mansion, I'll explain." Frank led the way.

Isolated in private rooms, Seth opened the safe and divided the cash on hand. "Here's your share. If you need more, I can get some from Ben and reimburse him when I go to the bank on Monday."

After Frank stuffed the currency in saddlebags he'd brought with him, he turned to leave, but stopped and said, "I'll keep in touch, pal."

"What's this life and death thing about?" Seth was not about to let his long-time companion, leave without reason.

"She's waiting out back ... my wife, Johnetta."

Having necessary justification, he hugged his ally and said, "God's speed. Take care of Johnetta. You know how to reach me if needed. You're truly my friend."

Frank's slim figure disappeared. Seth already missed the man who had been so much a part of his life for so long. But a new phase of existence had begun for him. He would continue the journey, not with Frank, but with Imogene by his side.

"Seth," Ola called from the entrance. "Ben's got a slight fever. Don't appear serious. But I would rest easy if the doctor saw him."

"Of course," he answered. Putting aside his mission, he ventured outside where dawn had fallen and mounted his stallion.

Once the physician attended Grandfather, Seth retired in one of the front parlors and waited. Lounging upon a sofa in the dark, thoughts naturally veered toward Imogene.

"You heartless creature," he whispered. "You've run from me again... . And now there wasn't any need to."

"I'm leaving now." The doctor stood near the exit. "Ben's resting. Nothing serious. Too much excitement today."

"Yes, it has been." Concern for Imogene returned.

No sooner had he seen the doctor out, and Ola requested he attend Ben while she rested. Undressing but for shirt and trousers, he stretched out beside the sleeping elder upon the spacious bed. Even though memories of his lover bombarded, he joined his grandfather in slumber.

***

Having settled in the home for unwed mothers, Imogene reviewed several household duties she must perform in lieu of payment. Now that there would be a life to care for, she must reserve what little money she'd saved and invested. Seth must never know of their offspring.

Sleep had not been easy after her arrival. She rose the next morning early, but weary. Having washed and dressed, she ventured in search of the community dinning area.

"Imogene," Miss Ida, the home's matron, called.

"Yes?" she responded, stopping just at the parlor.

"You're late. We run a strict program here. It must be well-regimented and no favoritism given."

Imogene could not believe her ears. This woman implied, because of her close relationship with Maude, that she expected special treatment and would not hold up her end of the rules.

"We only allow three infractions. This has been you first," the tall, gaunt woman, Ida, said.

"I'm sorry," Imogene replied, swallowing her pride. This woman's summation, completely wrong, had no basis. Hadn't she taken on, with sharing general household duties, mending and sewing for the other nine unwed mothers, there? But not wanting confrontation said, "It won't happen again."

"See that it doesn't, young woman." Ida's sallow skin deepened the wrinkles already etched around her lips and eyes.

Life would not be easy here, Imogene realized. Only until the baby's birth, she knew.

"Duties are waiting!" the matron declared, shattering Imogene's thoughts and prompting her haste toward the cooking area.

Passing days had accumulated into a week. And Imogene, exhausted from overwork; depressed at separation from friend, Maude, and, more than anything, her lover, Seth, considered leaving the place that seemed more prison than haven. But such mattered little.

"Only for you, my precious," she whispered to her unborn babe while rubbing her swollen middle. So determined, she must press on.

Friday had turned gray, almost black. Moisture prevalent in the air, indicated rain. After the noon repast of thick beef stew, baked bread and milk, she began cleaning.

This particular day her thoughts had continually turned to Seth. Formerly, he had solely invaded her dreams. As she stacked dishes and began drying them, Thoughts of him had intensified. She cringed at him and Johnetta intimate.

"Imogene," Bella, one of the unweds, whispered, giving blessed interruption. "There's a visitor asking for you."

"Maude!" she cried, running toward the parlor.

"Imogene?" someone said near the room's entrance.

Before she realized, he captured her lips with his own and held her close. "You said she didn't reside here." His voice, comforting, was still accusatory as he addressed Ida.

"Did you not tell me to admit no one but Maude Graves," Ida said.

"Yes," she admitted, unable to move from Seth's arms.

"Why?" he asked, almost pleading. "You run from me; break my heart. There was no need."

"Your marriage. I need no other reason. I've told you I'll never be your mistress." She tried to pull from his warmth.

"It's unseemly," Ida scolded. "I'll not have such conduct here, a home for mothers—"

Imogene prayed Seth had not, somehow, heard or understood Ida's words. As his gripe tightened around her body, she suspected he'd heard, and when his black eyes drilled into hers, she knew he had comprehended fully.

"How dare you keep this from me, woman!" he shouted.

Having never seen Seth this infuriated, something inside stirred, not fear, but a certain affinity flooded her soul. She could put no name to the emotion. But it welled up and spilled down her cheeks in the form of tears.

"You, sir, must leave ... now!" Ida squawked. "Get out!"

Imogene, unsettled, stood and watched Seth snatch his brown bowler from the table and slap it upon his trimmed mane. He nearly knocked over the small table where the hat had been. He would leave and never return. If she wanted him out of her life, why act as though she didn't?

"Get out, you!" Ida screamed, looking at Seth and pointing outside.

"We're both leaving," Seth said, pulling Imogene along; snatching a red shawl from the hall coat rack and forcing her outdoors. "Put this around you!" He put the wrap around her.

"But—but" was all Imogene could say in weak protest. What could she do, overwhelmed with his prowess?

"Let's go." Effortlessly, he picked her up and deposited her upon his stallion and climbed behind.

"I—I—" she protested, attempting to dismount.

"Quiet," he whispered in his deep, soft voice, encasing her in both arms. "Rest, Imogene. We'll talk later."

Yes, she was tired. Her head rested against his hardness. Secured, warm and safe she slumbered.

Awakening with the roar of thunder and lightening streaks, Imogene jumped and emitted a cry.

"We're nearly home," Seth whispered, holding her close.

Too near her lover; experiencing his heat and essence she remembered his married state. He knew their relationship must change. She looked into his smiling, contented face.

"Yes, my love?" he said, before she'd spoken.

"Seth, this can't be. Our association can't be."

He gave her a puzzled look.

"You must understand ... I can't, even as a friend, have further dealings with you." She felt awful, going back on their previous promise of friendship. How could she, being near, avoid intimacy with him? Impossible!

"Going back on your word?" He seemed to tease.

"I'm serious, Seth."

"And I'm still upset with you for not telling me about our unborn child." All play had left his features and voice. He stopped his horse. "You had no right, Imogene."

"I had to." She paused and tried to swallow bile welling inside. "You're married now. I didn't want to interfere."

"I'm not," he proclaimed.

"You lie!" She looked him squarely in the eye. "I saw and heard you say—"

"Evidently, you didn't hear Johnetta."

"No, but—"

"Listen, love, the way's clear. She's already wed."

"Unbelievable. She, so smitten with you, wed to another."

"What I've told you, my love, is truth." His gaze never wavered. "You do believe me?"

"Yes," she said, smiling up at him.

Rain began falling, drenching her locks and clothes. But she ignored the wet. It felt like cleansing to her soul.

"My love and bride," he whispered, giving her brief kisses with more invasive ones. "My heart, at last, is fulfilled."

"You have mirrored my sentiments," she uttered.

Sun burst forth. Warmth and light surrounded as their journey continued. Yes, tribulation had passed and jubilation arrived and Imogene and Seth would travel life's road together and in love.

EPILOGUE

"Mercy!" she emitted from between clenched teeth. And both palms, which she held tightly over her lips, muffled the word further.

"Stop acting like a mighty woman, child! You got every right to scream and cuss. You been laying here for ten hours saying nothing; just twisting and turning," Ola scolded.

"I want my husband," Imogene weakly demanded.

"That child ain't waitin' for Seth and no other man—or woman. Doctor's been called. He's on another birthing and will come when he can. Ain't never had no babe of my own, but I brung many into the world."

"I want my husband!" Imogene managed to shout. Ola's words and wide form, standing above her, hadn't given comfort.

"You know Seth went on important business three days ago. He's due back any minute."

Yes, she knew, and had seen him off, never shedding a tear, but praying he'd return before the birth. Pain had started that night, hardly nagging at first. But as time had progressed, discomfort gradually turned intense.

She held her breath, anticipating her body's natural response. So when torture came, she stifled her cries. And without warning, Ola pulled back the sheet and looked.

"Almost time," the older woman said. Compassion showed upon the elder woman's, suddenly sympathetic face.

Imogene only nodded, she felt her insides falling out and when her body contorted and screams erupted, she understood fully what labor meant.

"Push, child!" Ola coached, widening Imogene's already parted legs.

Doing as directed, she prayed the baby would deliver and end her pain. Never, in all her days, had she toiled so hard.

"Where is she?" a male voice called.

Not quite aware, Imogene, believing Seth had arrived, felt elated and, surprisingly, suffering lessened. But seeing the doctor, she lapsed back into misery and gripped Ola's hands.

"Nearly here," the doctor said calmly, barely rolling up his shirt sleeves. "All birthing should be so easy."

"Easy on who?" Imogene shouted, pushing harder than before because of rage, impatience and Seth's absence.

"Good, girl," Ola said as the doctor lifted a wiggling, wailing form. "It's a boy," she announced, wrapping the child and placing the newborn into Imogene's reaching arms. "You done Seth and all of us proud! We have a male child to carry on the Thomas name."

Imogene smiled in response. She'd finally acquired the older woman's acceptance. Now she felt like a family member. Cuddling the child close, she slept.

***

Someone had arrived. Her eyes adjusted to the light, and she sought her baby.

"We're here," came from across the room. Seth, holding their child in his arms, approached. "Didn't want to wake you, love." He sat near and planted kisses across her forehead and lips, saying, "Thank you, Imogene, my wife and lover, for this precious bundle, the product of our love."

Smiling and nestling close, she replied, "Thank you, my husband, partner and lover for the void you have filled in my heart ..."